'Her words knit a narrative ⟨...⟩
ultimately, freedom and a richer life. It is a love story between
a woman and her boat, and how Susan finds strength and
courage through sailing' *Practical Boat Owner*,
Best New Releases

ABOUT THE AUTHOR

Susan Smillie is a former *Guardian* journalist, and wrote mainly
on travel, food and the arts. She is the author of one previous
book, *The Last Sea Nomads*, published by Guardian Shorts. She is
based between Scotland, with her family, and Greece, where
her boat, *Isean*, is currently moored.

PENGUIN BOOKS

The Half Bird

Nominated for The Richard Jefferies Award for Best Nature Writing 2024

Financial Times Best Summer Travel Book of 2024

'Remarkable' *Scotsman*

'It's hard to read *The Half Bird* without wondering whether you could do it too. It may be better to start by pondering Smillie's wider message – that to work out what will truly make you happy, you first need to stop and smell the air around you' *Guardian*

'This tale of one woman's solo sail from Land's End to the shores of Greece has all the hallmarks of the [travel writing] genre, as the author quits her job to follow her dream and somehow stretches it out into a three-year voyage. With only the basics onboard, this soon turns into a thoughtful meditation on solitude, resilience and the irresistible lure of the sea' *Wanderlust Magazine*

'Smillie has written this beautiful, evocative, raw, occasionally even funny book about her decision to take off around Britain in her extremely bijou sailing boat *Isean* – and then turn left at Land's End instead' Felicity Cloake, author and *Guardian* columnist

'This book is for all nature lovers, freedom lovers and anyone who dreams of escaping the daily grind. Without a big budget or much experience, Susan makes her dream happen and takes to a life at sea. We travel with her through her solo journey, experiencing the highs and lows, the fear and loneliness as well as the joy and elation of being truly free. I would recommend it to anyone, sailor or not, who wants a life-affirming, moving and ⸺⸺⸺⸺⸺⸺⸺⸺⸺⸺⸺⸺ *One*

'There is a rare subtlety in so much of this. Smillie finds a freedom, beauty and joy in amongst the rolling waves and shifting tides of loss, illness and grief. *The Half Bird* is an immensely enjoyable ocean adventure, but what emerges is a deeply inspiring story about the quiet strengths that reside within us all' Will Millard, author and BBC presenter

'I didn't know a love song between a woman and her boat could transport, and transfix me. *The Half Bird* made my heart whole' Rhik Samadder, author of *I Never Said I Loved You*

'This is a book that will take us both of those places [Scotland and Greece] and many many more besides, it's a book full of beautiful imagery, it soars and it is grounded, which is a very very difficult thing to pull off. And it's a book that when I opened it, I felt it could have been written for me; it has sailing, it has adventure, it has a quest for the self, it has all of those things that I look for in a book. And it is adventurous' Wyl Menmuir, author of *The Draw of the Sea*

'If you read one piece of nature writing, travel writing or life writing this year — make it this one. With mediations on grief, minimalist living, womanhood and being childless by choice, it's so much more than a sailing memoir — it's writing at its most inspiring, most gentle, most beautiful. I adored every word' Claire Daverley, author of *Talking at Night*

'One of the world's great people has written one of the year's great books' Xan Brooks, author of *The Catchers*

'This thrilling journey of challenge and joy, of grief and being suddenly single, of boldness as she takes on each new horizon, underlines the simple fact that resilience builds the more we attempt' *Sainsbury's Magazine*

'Full of the adventure, joy and fear of setting to sea in a small boat' *Sailing Today*

The Half Bird

SUSAN SMILLIE

PENGUIN BOOKS

PENGUIN BOOKS

UK | USA | Canada | Ireland | Australia
India | New Zealand | South Africa

Penguin Books is part of the Penguin Random House group of companies
whose addresses can be found at global.penguinrandomhouse.com

Penguin Random House UK,
One Embassy Gardens, 8 Viaduct Gardens, London SW11 7BW

penguin.co.uk

Penguin
Random House
UK

First published by Penguin Michael Joseph 2024
Published in Penguin Books 2025
001

Typeset by Jouve (UK), Milton Keynes
Printed and bound in Great Britain by Clays Ltd, Elcograf S.p.A.

The authorized representative in the EEA is Penguin Random House Ireland,
Morrison Chambers, 32 Nassau Street, Dublin D02 YH68

A CIP catalogue record for this book is available from the British Library

ISBN: 978-0-241-55317-6

Penguin Random House is committed to a sustainable future for our business, our readers and our
planet. This book is made from Forest Stewardship Council® certified paper.

for

Kate & Sam

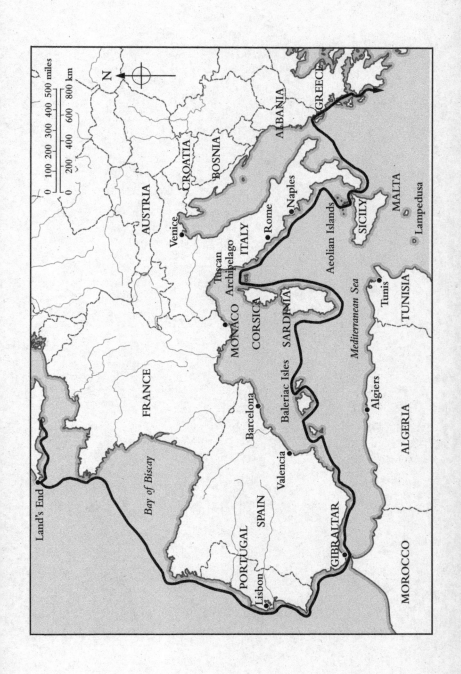

I.

Isean is soaring. Wing on wing, snowy white against Jurassic skies. Cliffs packed with relics, traces and tracks, fossils and footprints. Tiny dinosaurs glide on gale-force winds. A sky full of birds. They angle just so, feathers flattened to the gusts. Ascending updraughts, riding currents. Brilliant and bright, the time of their lives. The wind is rushing, the gulls are screaming. A raucous gathering in a storm. I'm flying too, eyes wide, heart lifting, breathing it in. All that air. There's no one here to break the spell, to crash this party. No one to stop us.

We're above and apart. Up with the birds. I've never known this kind of release, this boundless joy. A sense that I've found it, the untold story, about happiness and freedom, and life really giving. That it can be simple. I found something. It was nothing. An absence of something. A yawning empty horizon. No rules or restraints. No one with their better way of how to go. The only way my own. The freedom of that. It rushes and lifts and just overruns you. To belong, unfathomably, right here, in this wild place. We climb higher, we dip lower, we lean with the breeze, judging the gusts. The wind force builds and bends the bluff. *Isean* responds with grace and with calm, steady she goes. As with the birds, their breastbones like keels, she is made to glide. On the wind, through the waves. Her sails flattened, her hull carving white horses. As joyful as me. We are sailing.

A quarter of a mile off in a collision of cliffs and sea, there's a raging line of surf. The English Channel churning powerfully, bright foaming crests like teeth untethered, tumbling over sea green. A confused mess of steep waves. I stare in sudden and quiet horror, scan the horizon from the headland out to sea, searching without luck for a break in the frothing line. St Alban's tidal race, turbulent overfalls stretching as far as the eye can see. Some fifteen miles on the other side of this barrier lies sandy Weymouth, our destination. Now it feels like a distant dream, approachable as Atlantis. The joy, the freedom, the sense of belonging – gone. What in the world am I doing? I don't know. I don't remotely belong here. I don't know what to do. My friend Saoirse is with me, in her early twenties, on her third ever sail. I'm calm on the surface, like a swan on a lake, feet kicking below. Nerves building, I consider our options. We could turn around, but with the tide against us, we won't make it back to Poole before nightfall, a place of narrow channels and grounding sandbanks I'd rather not navigate in the dark.

'It's going to get rough,' I say. 'Hand on the boat at all times.'

My stomach is lurching, my heart thuds as the building swell pummels *Isean*'s hull. We are going into the tidal race.

The better choices were the ones I had failed to make. I should have timed our westbound arrival to coincide with high tide at Dover, when the water calms a little here. I could divert four miles to sea and bypass the race, or head inland, weaving round the rocks on the inner passage that runs more gently, but a nerve-wracking fifty metres offshore. If anything goes wrong – snagging a lobster pot, losing steering – you're right on the rocks. It calls for calm conditions and a confident skipper; we have gale-force winds gusting against the tide . . . and me. In any case, I don't know these options. In my jaunts day-sailing along the south coast, I had remained blissfully – shamefully – unaware of tidal races. Now, I would be relying on beginner's luck and my small, sturdy boat to get us through this, the most sobering sailing lesson I've ever had.

I had set off west in a kind of madness weeks earlier. Friends had casually mentioned plans for a week's sailing out of Brixham and I made it a mission to join them. I dreamed of sky and sea. A disquiet had been forming; life in the city had become oppressive and I needed air. It was a realisation that came gradually, then rushed all at once, overnight, like a dawn chorus rousing me out of a stupor. I responded, ran south, exited the stifling city in a flood of instinct, seeking the salt and space, the silver and blue of a shape-shifting sea. I had always loved the water but hadn't sailed until my thirties. I was an amateur with a day-skipper qualification, and I longed to put my knowledge of theoretical navigation into practice, plan proper passages, try anchoring – all the things real sailors do. Suddenly, with the prospect of joining my friends in Brixham, I envisaged myself doing so under the guidance of experienced sailors in idyllic Devon bays. In my excitement, I'd glossed over the details of how I'd get there. I lacked experience, I failed to plan, but I did have an excellent little boat. It was my ex-boyfriend Phil who found *Isean* in our last year together. She'd been languishing in a boatyard on the west coast of Scotland for years – a real project. But what beautiful lines! A Nicholson 26, a long keel, a true classic. I made all the mistakes everyone makes when they fall in love with a boat – the first, technically, was buying her. At a fraction of the cost of most second-hand cars, she seemed cheap in the misleading way boats do to a novice. She was a mess outside and a shell inside: there were thousands to spend. But what a feeling to rescue such a beautiful boat from ruin – worth more than money. And now she's kin.

She came to Brighton on the back of a truck. That featureless strip of channel between Shoreham and Seaford made for safe learning – lots of space and depth, not much to hit. If there were too many white horses at sea we wouldn't venture out, happy to enjoy the boat on her mooring. But I'd wistfully watch sailing boats arrive, salt-crusted sails dropping on the way in, decks glistening with sea spray, crew spilling out in all their gear – rosy-faced, healthily tousled – all big grins, heading for well-earned showers and dinner. And off they'd go in the morning, on their way out to sea again, their boats doing what boats are meant to do. I began to look at *Isean* differently. She seemed subdued, this seaworthy boat, her potential wasted on our modest day sails. She was capable of so much more and I was desperate to sail her as she should be sailed.

On New Year's Eve 2014, I made my only resolution. I would learn to sail my little boat. I spent the first months of 2015 revising navigation, and on a misty April morning, I set off with Phil, by now a dear friend. We were bound west, for somewhere more challenging. 'If you can sail in the Solent,' people had said, 'you can sail anywhere.' By Easter, with help, we were there. I had expected a busy stretch of water but was still taken aback at the volume of marine traffic and the impressive number of hazards. Sailing around this ship-filled strait was an exercise in concentration, the horizon intermittently blotted out by one giant or another. Cruise ships like gleaming cities floating past, tiny balconies with matchstick figures piled up into the air. Stern steel navy ships under way. Lego-like cargo ships, stacked high with coloured containers. Sunday racers and romantic old tall ships, sails crowding blue skies like a Glasgow tenement laundry day. There were the tankers, tugs and trawlers, tour boats, ferries and hovercraft, speeding in and out of Portsmouth and Southampton. And a multitude of invisible obstacles – man-made defence walls running undersea like piratical freight trains, and natural barriers such as the Brambles, a lumbering sandbank slowly edging west. But these were nothing compared to the Solent's strongest force – a help or a hindrance, depending on what you're doing. It's tides that are king here, rushing between the Isle of Wight and the mainland with the strong winds that also funnel through. The tides dictate your movements above all else; you need to carefully time your passages with, not against them, especially with a small engine that can't compete with their power. There's the unique phenomenon of a double high water too. Great if you love tides! Hurray, more tides!

I was never a stickler for rules in life. 'You always have to try an unlocked door,' Phil would sigh as I blithely ignored 'no entry' signs or dragged him around abandoned places in the middle of nowhere. At sea, where rules mattered, I converted fast. The collision regulations I'd struggled to memorise took on real and urgent meaning. When learning, I'd cursed the finicky detail of different buoys and beacons, colours and light sequences; now I was filled with admiration for the systems that made such practical sense at sea. I'd find myself in the dark, squinting at flashes, wondering when 'quick' becomes 'very quick' . . . or wait, is that 'continuous'? I'd test myself on flags and candy-striped red-and-white safety marks. I was the world's happiest swot on the most educational fairground ride ever. I got used to the proximity of other boats, learned how fast ships advanced and where to be in relation to them; when to hold my nerve and when to shift. I learned to think much farther ahead after sailing with my friend Gary Bettesworth, a professional skipper I would call upon several times over the years. 'It would be prudent to tack,' he'd say, anticipating the movements of others. Prudent became my guiding principle. If I wasn't sure – or a bit lazy – about the necessity of moving, I'd decide it would be prudent, then do it, beaming like a head girl at Sea Cadets. I took it all in, made my mistakes; after a season, I started to feel reasonably competent.

Sailing came late but boats had always been in my peripheral vision, quietly working their way into my dreams. There was an old wooden hull in our garden when I was tiny; a hulking great thing, it seemed to me. A place to run when Billy, our hissy gander, chased me, his epic wings flapping, long neck snaking as my little feet clambered the ladder to safety. I grew up in Dumbarton, a town of geese-guarded distilleries with a rich maritime heritage. A place forever bound with ships and whisky bottles. It was home to one of the most beautiful boats in the world today – the *Cutty Sark*, built on the River Leven in 1869; the fastest tea clipper of her time. She's now in Greenwich, her copper hull gleaming like gold behind glass. In a half bottle, she flies through London air. A few miles upriver from Dumbarton, in the shipyards of Clydebank, Edgar, my grandfather on my dad's side, was one of those hand-riveting the *Waverley* in the 1940s. In his heavy moleskin trousers, cotton in his ears – no safety gear back then. His work must have been sound. That beautiful little ship now claims to be the world's last paddle steamer to take passengers to sea.

My dad lives in Dunoon now, a town to the west, where the Clyde opens out and pushes south towards the isles of Bute, Arran and the Irish Sea. My parents moved there twenty years ago, the last of a series of flits orchestrated by my mum. She was a gypsy at heart, would have loved to travel, but raising three kids – Stephen and David and me – filled a couple of decades. She and my dad considered a move to Spain when I was a teenager, but she wouldn't leave her own mother, Maw Joss, a regular fixture in the calendar of family life. Instead, she got her nomadic fix dreaming outside estate agent windows, always an eye on a new location. She got a buzz from moving home, shifting my dad from place to place; a small profit on each wreck he renovated bought something better. In the nineties they moved briefly to Ireland, but she missed family. I'd left Dumbarton for London at nineteen, happy to visit my parents in Galway or Glasgow, but my brothers lived in Scotland, and by the time I'd finally got myself off to the University of Sussex at twenty-four, my parents had returned to a house right on the banks of Loch Long in Arrochar.

There were special times together in those years. I'd be home for key moments, for Hogmanays when Stephen's folk band, Shenanigan, incited boisterous gatherings under Scottish night skies that hardly knew how to get dark, a fast and furious blur of music and laughter that petered out to the birdsong of dawn. Stephen was always in the middle of it, head tilted above his accordion, his features knitted in musical concentration. I mostly remember my mum's face in the early hours, sober and smiling, good-natured and gently steering us all off to bed. Stephen and my dad had a little motorboat and they'd take it around the lochs, Stephen diving for shellfish on a safety line. I remember his stories, delivered with good-natured exasperation, of how he'd be poised on the seabed, clutches of gleaming mussels just within grasp, when suddenly he'd be hoicked up, his fingers stretching impotently as my dad reeled him back to the surface.

What we couldn't have known was how limited our time together would be. Shortly after my parents returned to Scotland, we lost Stephen. Suddenly, violently, my eldest brother was gone. A car crash ended his life at thirty-two. I was just finishing my first-year exams, the whole summer ahead. My dad called, his voice cracking on the phone. I recall a numb journey to a house suffocating in the first wave of grief, my nights spent on the shores of Loch Long with a bottle of whisky, talking to the sky, where I thought Stephen might be. Relatives and friends came and went, love and kindness carried in the pots of food, rounds of tea, hot toddies nursed. There were shared stunned silences, sleepless nights spent in tears and conversation, laughter and stories. Stephen was present – in his rightful place at the centre of the gathering, but inexplicably in the past, no longer bringing the room to life with that astute wit, with the music, energy – *craic* – that drew others to him like moths to a candle. I was afraid of the silence; with Stephen's music and his articulate din suddenly gone, the family was fractured. I felt inadequate, quiet, dull. I had no idea how we would fill that vacuum – as if anyone wanted a replacement.

The grief eclipsed everything except my parents' agony, the enormity of it cutting through even my own pain. My dad was lost in something unfathomable, seemed bewildered by the depth of his suffering. My mum almost died. For a moment in those first days, she turned to the wall. I remember it clearly. I didn't know back then that her resources were already depleted; that, privately and quietly, she was facing her own mortality, the brutal matter of breast cancer. Her stoicism kept this from us for many years. A heavy weight for her and my dad to carry. I wish I'd had the chance to offer support but she wanted to protect us. It was probably a form of protection for her too, to cope in private. Most of all I think it was a kind of optimistic 'screw you' – a determination that her life should continue as normal, that she would not be cast as a victim. When Stephen died, though, she wanted to go too. She held on, for us; took the harder path, in surviving. Her firstborn child. I remember stories of Stephen as a little boy, my mum absent-mindedly wandering off, another kid hanging on to her. 'You've got the wrong boy's hand,' he'd cried. 'So special,' she told me. In those first days, she articulated the immensity of her grief in a few devastating words. 'So special, your first child.' After that, she would always walk out and look over the water before she went to bed, saying goodnight to her boy.

Dunoon was the last place my mum lived, the last place she brought my dad, the place I said goodbye to her, the place I go to him now. In the summer, the *Waverley* is often there; seventy-five years on, inevitable as the tides, this little ship coming and going. I swim there when I return, seeking solace in the cold water, porpoises rolling, cormorants circling, each stroke pulling me to the Gantocks lighthouse where the steamer paddles and the seals sing. Through rain and sunshine I go, and best of all, through shifting mist. In the fog, I'd hear the boat before I saw her, the puffs of steam; a wet sound, like the seals snorting, the beating of her giant paddle wheels. A gentle rhythm from a bygone age, the sound of home and kin, of belonging; a sound that, like the muffled call of foghorns on the coast, clings to the landscape and belongs to its people.

Gradually, her lines take shape out of the haze; the elegant curves, the warm timber. Even on the bleakest of days, through rain, through your own tears, you can't see this boat without smiling. And I saw her, this old friend, on the south coast of England. A good omen, just off Christchurch, and just before my journey west. She was chugging cheerfully along. My heart lifted in recognition. So touching to sail with her here, everything shifting yet solid and familiar. The past and present colliding, home and family connected; the world made smaller, manageable – navigable. I wonder what Edgar would have made of these, my first steps on the water. I didn't really get to know him, this man's man. He died while I was young and before that, I was too scared to talk to him. He loved weans, I'm told, but I was timid and he seemed as tough as the white-hot rivets he once hammered into place. I expect he would have been startled at the sight of two women on a little boat in that big sea off St Alban's Head. I can imagine his furrowed brow, chin jutting in justified concern at my lack of experience too. I shouldn't have been there – of course I shouldn't. I'd been driven on that journey west by a determination that bordered on obsessive. What had started as a loose plan suddenly ignited, in a direct reaction to Brexit.

I was in a marina near Deptford for the referendum, on another old boat that was my home. I had that rarest of London things, a close-knit community around me. Saoirse had moved onto a neighbouring boat the previous winter. I remember her arrival – a big grin in a woolly hat, always on her bike, her voice blasting across the dock like a foghorn. She was bright, funny, almost half my age, with a teenage vernacular that belied great maturity. 'It is indeed "sick",' I'd nod at her enthusiasm for skateboarding or the Shambala Festival. In turn, she laughed at my teenage tendencies, my focus firmly on fun while most women my age were deep in kids. We fast became friends, the two of us single, enthusing about boats and the sea. Life was good in our microcosm, but the surrounding atmosphere had been tense for weeks: families, colleagues and friends all on one side of the vote or the other. It had been strange to witness the evolution of the referendum, a Pandora's jar for Little Britain. This dry constitutional matter wouldn't interest the general public, the thinking seemed to go, even as the monster took shape before our eyes. In no time it dominated everything, a highly charged debate about identity that unleashed so much anger and emotion it often defied rational discussion. The lead-up to the vote saw PR stunts and headline-grabbing claims paraded on buses and boats, from the infamous '£350 million for the NHS' slogan to the mad spectacle of a Leave and Remain flotilla trading insults via megaphones on the Thames. I missed Stephen at times like this. He would have laughed at the insanity of the political circus, but he would also have been doing something constructive.

He'd completed his law degree just before he died, intending to specialise in human rights. His finest skill was one I lack – where I take time to gather my thoughts, Stephen was fast-thinking, an articulate and persuasive speaker. He wore his knowledge lightly and had a rare ability to reach out to others, taking on opposing views with a warmth that charmed and disarmed. He was maddening at times, in the way that he'd see straight to the core of you, to the weak link in your chain. But he did it with empathy, with knowing humour, offering himself up to ridicule, so you'd end up laughing, closer than ever. This easy approach was something many of us seemed to lack at a time it was badly needed. I was deeply frustrated at my own verbal paralysis as I watched everything unfold with a Munchian scream sliding down my face.

We seemed to retreat further into tribes. For once, media reports of a country divided were not hyperbole. On 16 June we were confronted with Nigel Farage's anti-migrant poster: 'take back control of our borders' across a mass of black and brown faces, the words 'BREAKING POINT' screaming in red capitals. A few hours later, the country reeled in horror at news of the brutal murder of Jo Cox at the hands of a far-right terrorist. Cox was a Labour MP, best known for her humanitarian work, for campaigns on loneliness and immigrant rights. She also supported remaining in the EU. It happened on the twentieth anniversary of Stephen's death. I always say dates don't affect me but evidence suggests otherwise. In my twenties I temporarily lost my licence for driving drunk on what would have been Stephen's birthday. In my forties, ten years on from my mum's death, I sobbed as an osteopath eased the tension my back was holding so tightly. It is often my shallow breathing that reminds me what time of year it is. Our bodies retain memories. Grief finds a way to assert itself. And when you're already depleted, your capacity for dealing with the hard stuff of life is diminished. Raw with feeling in that bleak week, I read of Jo, a mother who lived with her young family on a boat on the Thames. I listened to the mournful sound of ships' foghorns just two miles upriver, a collective wail of pain and grief, sounded by those in her community – an extended family, I imagined. The shock of it all silenced the terrible racket for a short time. Everything felt fractured.

After voting to remain, I was up early with a sense of foreboding, watching rolling reports as news of Brexit broke.

The significance of the result was palpable. Saoirse messaged, despondent, from her boat. We'd been in the habit of taking our kayaks out before work. I switched off the television, paddled out to the middle of the dock, where we sat in companionable silence, absorbing it all. From a barge, a neighbour called out, 'The prime minister's resigned.' It was not yet 9 a.m. Back on board, I dressed for work at the *Guardian* newspaper as anger and dismay poured out online from like-minded friends and colleagues. I knew what the office would be like, the atmosphere heavy and glum. My job — concerned with food features — would be entirely pointless. And it was a Friday. With a sudden and selfish certainty, I made a decision that was at once irresponsible and unprofessional. I sent Saoirse one word: 'Sailing'. Then we were on a train heading south to *Isean*. By the afternoon we were at sea, outside Gosport in twenty-five knots of wind, beginning the journey that carried us to that tidal race. I fought the halyard — the line that lifts the mainsail — which had whipped itself into a tangle round the mast as Saoirse learned — fast — how to steer. We headed up the River Hamble and that evening we crashed noisily through the pub doors of the Jolly Sailor. Overhearing conversations, we remembered Brexit had happened — this momentous thing that had dominated for so long had been blown out of our minds. We had been caught up in the sea, the stinging wind, the heeling boat, laughing and shouting with rope-whipped hands; the physical and mental exertion and the exhilaration. The sheer joy of it. That morning now felt a world away. I didn't know it then, but 24 June 2016 was the day that my life completely changed direction. Stephen would have cheered.

Over the next few weekends I dragged various people aboard to help me west. Phil joined from Beaulieu to Poole on a fine July day with sparkling blue seas. We passed Hurst Point, looking south as the Isle of Wight's westernmost point hove into view. Out there, the Needles, that ragged row of incisors gleaming white and harking to the west. Drama in spades, but what struck me more than the atmospheric scenery was the space, a world apart from the busy Solent; an alternate universe to London. Ahead, a vast and glorious expanse of empty water. No other boats in sight. I felt my shoulders drop. With the leeway around the boat, there was now room in my mind – clear, quiet, calm. And conditions were perfect. The sun was shining, a few fluffy clouds were bumped along by the gentle breeze that also pushed us west. I went below deck, glanced at the charts, unhurriedly made lunch, staring out at the glassy water we glided through – a peace I'd forgotten. By the time we arrived at Poole, my feet trailed in the water, like the Brighton days, but I was now marvelling at a rolling Dorset landscape that felt so well earned. It was brilliant – all stress gone. A week later Saoirse and I were at St Alban's Ledge.

It's messy, intimidating but doable, I decide. I'm apprehensive but not scared – I know my boat is solid. I trust her. I start the engine for extra power and control. Off we go, into the roaring race, and then it's too late to change my mind; it's a case of staying calm and holding on. I'm helming as best I can through steep, heavy waves. Normally, at five tons, *Isean* cuts easily through rough water. Now, she's pointing up, bow to sky, then bellyflopping into troughs that feel like chasms in the sea. I have a feeling of weightlessness, my stomach lurching on the drop. The noise of it! How can water feel this solid? Waves are rushing the gunwales, but my worst fear – swamping the cockpit – doesn't materialise. Saoirse is standing beside me, holding on, facing forward. I'm feeling irresponsible for putting her in this situation. But she's fine as long as I'm fine. And I'm fine as long as the boat's fine. Which it is. In fact, both Saoirse and *Isean* look like they're having the time of their lives. I'm having a private ordeal. There is a huge wave coming now.

I push the tiller over to scull at an angle. We climb and suddenly we're flying down the other side to the steepest drop yet. My stomach feels like it's hitting the seabed. Still dry in the cockpit. One more; we are up and over it. 'That's as bad as it's going to get,' I say. I have no idea why I say this with such certainty, but it turns out to be true. Those two formidable waves were probably the 'stopping line' I will read about the following day. After this, it's over fast; in about twenty minutes we're spat out the other side. Saoirse is rosy and glowing, her eyes sparkling, an enormous grin cracking her face. 'Wicked,' she bellows. I manage a thin smile.

Weymouth beckons, its Georgian terraces and esplanade, its gentle curve of sand. I'll regret rushing this stunning Jurassic Coast. I don't yet know that I won't return to enjoy the beauty of Old Harry Rocks, Lulworth's perfect omega-shaped cove, the uncanny drama of Durdle Door. Today I've had enough drama. We push towards this landscape of chalk and green. It's all big-picture stuff at first, ordered patches of colour where ploughed fields and meadows nudge woodlands, cliffs give way to curving grassy hillsides, made familiar from hours of staring. Gradually, the town emerges, a welcome crop of hard buildings springing up from the softness of the land. Slowly, more details, sharper structures, just suggestions – at this distance size is impossible to judge and imagination fills in the rest. I'm seeking out solid harbour walls, the red and green markers to the sheltered channel I know is there. I've never wanted to get somewhere so badly. We head in just before dark, the sail drooping in big messy folds, lines looping like the hangman's noose, boom careening drunkenly from side to side.

What a special kind of relief it is to arrive in a safe harbour after such a sail. It doesn't matter that you've never been to this place before, for you are home. This is the peculiarity and privilege of arriving by boat. You're neither local nor tourist, but more than a visitor. Blown in by the wind, you're a mariner, part of an ancient tradition. It's something too about the welcome you get. Help from the harbour master or other boats, fellow sailors who stop and catch your ropes, understanding your fatigue, knowing your relief. They offer hands and a friendly word, then leave you to take care of your boat, get her sails away, put her to bed. She's looked after you, and you look after her. We get moored up, tidy the worst of the mess, seek out hot showers – heaven – and the nearest pub. I'm sitting there like a zombie amongst the racket of a Weymouth Saturday night in full swing, my eyes still wide with waves, my body pumped with the memory of it. I'm feeling contrite. There she is, my big-hearted friend, turning from the bar, with a couple of pints, a big smile on her face. We are showered, we have food coming. We are safe. 'All right, mate,' she grins, handing me my beer. My heart is so full of love for her at this moment I can't properly express it. 'I'm so glad I didn't drown you,' I say, as we knock glasses in happy cheers.

Someone once said that if you read all the pilot books you'd never leave the harbour. There's truth in that – scrutinising them can make for sleepless nights, and you rarely encounter the worst conditions they warn you about. But I'd always read them. Before a passage I'd check wind strength, direction and wave height, then turn to my almanac for tidal strength and flow, closely reading up on the harbour approaches. Then I'd scan my charts – if I found no obstructions and conditions were fair, I'd assume the deep sea was benign. Big mistake. That classic beginner's thing – you simply don't know how much you don't know. With knowledge comes caution. Reading back over the relevant section, there it was, St Alban's Ledge. Looking again at the charts, I saw the modest wave lines that indicate overfalls, tiny squiggles – so subtle! – but every mark on a chart means something and wave symbols ought to have stood out. The stupidity of it burned my face. Still, I'd got there, to this pretty town – I was inordinately grateful and might as well enjoy it. Sitting in Weymouth harbour – my favourite kind, right in the heart of things – felt like going back in time, men singing sea shanties by the quay, a fish auction under way. It was the start of the annual seafood festival, the sun was shining and all was well. Saoirse was gone and I was now part of the landscape as visitors strolled by with their ice creams, taking photographs and smiling down at me.

Just along the quay I noticed a young woman. She was striking – athletic, tanned, tattooed, blonde; adeptly weaving barefoot from boat to boat, tide charts in one hand, a rollie in the other, a broad grin. Her boat was even smaller than *Isean*. I wandered up to the pub in the evening for a pint and spotted her in animated Brexit conversation. 'Dad! Question everything!' She looked exasperated. 'I'm going to the loo and when I come back we're going to stop talking about this.' As she took off I made eye contact with her father. 'You're having the conversation that's taking place all over the country,' I observed, smiling. Eric, a gentle man with kindly eyes, raised his eyebrows: 'Debbie always says, "Let's stop talking about it," but it's her that always brings it up!'

I laughed as Debbie returned. Conversationally, we moved on. She'd noticed us coming in the day before. 'Pretty impressive to take on St Alban's Ledge in a gale,' she'd thought. 'No!' I immediately confessed, all guilt and shaken confidence. They went easy on me. It was a big lesson; I'll be more cautious. It was like a healing balm, confiding in experienced sailors who didn't pass judgement. Part of the learning curve, we agreed. I started to forgive myself a bit. They were sailing west too, each on their own boat. Debbie, a fine art graduate in her thirties, had the whole summer free. Given how little it costs to live on anchor, she said, she could subsidise the months roaming on what she earned working odd jobs over the winter. Somewhere a lightbulb went on in my mind. The following day, as I headed for the train to London, I saw them, bobbing happily in the sun, no doubt planning their passage across Lyme Bay, or arguing about Brexit. 'Back to work for me,' I called, grimacing. 'Don't go,' Debbie laughed. I shrugged in reply – 'Commitments!' – and ambled off reluctantly. But she had planted a seed.

2

White bubbles fizzed in celebration at *Isean*'s bow; we rushed along in the dark. We'd just left Weymouth to cross Lyme Bay, my first overnight sail and, at forty miles, the longest passage to date. I was on a high. With my friend Gary's help, I'd navigated the mighty Portland Bill, 'the most dangerous extended area of broken water in the English Channel', according to the *Shell Channel Pilot*. Chesil Beach, the long spit of 'cisel' flint and chert that stretches west from the Isle of Portland, was once known for the numerous bodies that washed up, boats shipwrecked on the rocky seabed below. Which is why Thomas Hardy called it Deadman's Bay. He knew this coast intimately; me not so much. I'd prepared in advance by watching videos of titanic seas roaring behind the unmistakable red and white stripes of Portland Bill lighthouse. As terrifying as they were, the films offered welcome relief from the political fallout of Brexit, the news cycle a psychodrama no one wanted to watch. I had run off to the vast sky, the shrill call of terns, the put-put of fishing boats, the wind and space, the sea – the sea! – and its cold stinging spray. It was exactly what I needed. My head was full of tidal streams, my lungs full of salty air, my heart recharged. I left Weymouth train station and there was my girl, waiting against the wall. I was so happy that I called out to greet her – 'Hey, *Isean*!' – without a care who heard. Gary arrived and we set off for the inshore passage at slack tide, a route that ran so alarmingly close to land we could see the expressions of passing ramblers. The sea felt big, swollen with a weird kind of energy but far from the violence of St Alban's. The kind of anticlimax you hope for. An important lesson in passage-planning. From there, we set off across a sparkling Lyme Bay, all wheeling gulls and silver water, the pungent whiff of brine.

As daylight faded, Gary went below to sleep, leaving me to my first watch and a sinking sun, burnt-orange and cinnamon clouds bruising the skies above. I was joined in the gloam by dolphins. As the darkness descended and the first stars punctured the sky, they reappeared, in a show of pure magic. Racing through bioluminescent water in streaks of light, diving and breaching, whistling and clicking. Glowing. The wildest of company, an otherworldly nightscape. How can we live within reach of such beauty and not know it? Simple chemistry, extraordinary things all around that we just miss. There is more magic in nature than we could ever dream. Everything felt closer, more intense in the dark: the iodine smell and taste on my skin, the warm breeze and heady rush of water, my eyes swimming with stars. I was lost in the big stuff, my thoughts free-floating up above the mast where the constellations were doing their own ordinary-extraordinary thing.

One of the weird aspects of grief is the predictability of its stages. When we lost Stephen, I remember wishing I could lose an arm, a leg, to have him back. Strange, I thought, but it was right there, in descriptions of the process – somewhere among the denial, anger, depression, there's bargaining. Inevitably, eventually, I came to acceptance. I determined that the pain of losing him would not eclipse the joy of knowing him, that I'd have a part of him with me on the journey, a part of me forever shaped by his example. Even as a child he showed character, befriending the kids who were bullied in his class. No small thing at a tender age to stand against the coming tide. He had the charisma and courage to do so throughout life. As an adult, he had boundless energy and approved of adventure. I knew he'd be raging if I didn't get out there and properly live. That is a daunting prospect when you're struggling. When you're just a bit safer down there in the dark, it's hard to see a path to somewhere brighter. I didn't know that grief would so thoroughly destroy my confidence. That I'd be so frightened by the thought of returning to normal life. The idea of embracing change – even for a better future – seemed too much to bear when simply making it to the shop without breaking down was a challenge. At the time, people said it would get better. But I did not want it to get better. I didn't want life to move on, for my brother's terrible, unnatural absence to become normal. I didn't want to keep growing older without him, to get to his age, and – how could it be possible – to grow older than him. But we have no idea how much resilience there is inside until we have to draw on it. That we crave happiness like plants lean to the light.

Stephen would have loved this change of direction, the nautical turn my life was taking. I had eclipsed the bad-tempered soundtrack of 2016 with the simple wonder of nature, all that beauty around me. I'd put my well-being first at a time when things were again looking bleak. It would have been so easy to get lost otherwise, thrown into an unhealthy cycle – work, sleep, work, drink, forget. I'd been there before, in the years after Stephen's death, when alcohol was a crutch and too many nights passed in a drunken blur. Partying is normal in your twenties, but my drinking was too fast, too hard; my need for company came from too great a fear of being alone. I didn't have the inner resources for sitting with myself, with all the sadness; didn't know what to do with it. When nights out with friends ended, an unhealthy habit formed – I carried on drinking, and found I preferred the quietness of this time alone to think with emotional distance. The alcohol helped to slant my grief in a more philosophical direction, made it bearable. It numbed and distorted it. Blind drunk, mad with grief, I would speak to Stephen; sometimes I'd convince myself that there was a positive in all that bleakness – I can talk to him whenever I want now. Sometimes drinking replaced a confidence I'd once had. I'd lost trust in the world, an innocence that you don't know to cherish when you're young, when your loved ones are just there. I was scared to be happy for a long time, superstitiously nervous if things started to feel too good, lest another phone call shatter my world.

Bad news doesn't always come on the phone, though. Phil and I were living in a flat in Brighton when my parents came for Christmas. They must have felt so burdened, trying to find the right time to tell me. They cornered me – I remember my alarm, moths in my stomach, fluttering with dread, as it dawned on me something was wrong. My mum came into my room with a quiet intent. I remember the gravity on her face, my sensation of panic, wanting to bolt. I must have known something was wrong. The signs were there – she was thin, but her gung-ho attitude and strength of character obliterated any physical frailty. And I hadn't wanted to see it. My dad was behind, closing the door, as she took control, delivering this blow in the gentlest way possible, a mother wounded, still protecting her young. She'd been dealing with breast cancer for over ten years by then. She must have watched me spinning around for all of those years, waited until I had some stability in my life before telling me. Once I was settled with Phil, that time had come.

We were lucky, we had three years left, spent in a rush of trips north, daily calls home. If my mum was good, I'd have a good day; if not, I'd be consumed with worry. She would know that, for she always sounded good, whatever kind of day she'd had. Phil carried me through those years; solid and unwavering, he balanced reality with optimism as we all focused on the things that helped – good diet, exercise, meditation – alongside my mum's treatment. I lived somewhere between terror and hope. In incremental steps, I faced the inevitable fact that we were losing her. We didn't waste the time. In dying, Stephen had taught us to love fully and openly, not to leave things unsaid. I remember a lot of laughter in those years: my mum, so strong and positive, preparing us somehow, without our knowing, with her lightness of touch, reminding us of the unbearable beauty, the fragile gift that is life. Yes, life is hard, she said, but you get out, look for light. She made time for beauty. We took a trip to the Isle of Skye, joined on the crossing by a minke whale. I remember her smiling down at this graceful creature, all gentle intelligence, its white belly on show as it turned to examine the ferry. There were nights when we danced like old-timers to bluegrass, bendy knees and crying with laughter. Her wit and capacity for fun were enormous. When I was a twenty-year-old, living in London, she arrived suddenly to nurse me through a small fever. She came by herself. We'd always been close. As I grew up, my parents were like friends. Sam and Kate, we called them, a habit Stephen started. Even so, I hadn't spent so much time with my mum outside of the family, free of her maternal role. In my London life I saw a different side to her. Once I was better, she joined in with me and my mates, with our dinner and dancing and daft conversations. Fun and silly and carefree. I remember being tipsy, all of us lying on the floor holding hands, talking about song lyrics and love. She must have been younger than I am now. I imagine what it would be like to take her out on *Isean*, to show her what I've learned. I imagine her with us now. She would approve of me finding joy out there in the dark. Rushing the night on a starlit deck. I had found my element. By the time my watch came to an end I was feeling everything far too intensely to sleep. I just lay there in wonder, listening to the creaking and groaning, the wind and the water; feeling the motion of the boat. A few hours later, as the sun rose, we sailed into Brixham under a pale-pink sky; I'd made it to the beautiful west.

There are times in life – rare and wonderful times – when you're exactly where you're meant to be. When things feel so entirely as they should that nothing can go wrong. You're on form, confident and happy, exuding positive energy, attracting good people, good things, eyes and smiles turned towards you. You can feel it in the air and you can feel it in yourself. I had acted in my own interests and was rewarded. What a joy to be in Devon in July. Brixham was busy with locals in summer mode — schoolchildren in wetsuits jumping off the quay, retired folk walking their dogs in prams; everyone smiling, reflecting my own happy state. Sitting in my cockpit, I consulted the charts ahead of what I hoped would be a relaxed jaunt round Berry Head; the only hazard appeared to be 'Bastard Rks' just off the tip. Fair enough, I'd keep well clear of those. Sailing into Dartmouth I was struck by the colour of that vivid little town, at its best on a sunny day approached from the sea. Everything — the birds and trees, the architecture and the river — seemed to radiate brilliance. We meandered on, past the handsome houses on the water's edge. I peered through narrow gaps where medieval streets climb to fields and orchard paddocks behind. I moored beneath Dittisham, where the river is quieter, greener and completely idyllic. Up there it's flanked by thick wooded hills teeming with birdlife — statuesque herons and wading oystercatchers. I sat still for hours looking for otters, lost in birdsong, brought back into a gentle version of the modern world by the huffing of the old steam train that chugs its way from Paignton. First you see the puffs of smoke, painting the green woods in charcoal clouds, then there's the friendly locomotive, shiny black and green, whistling and hissing its way along the sloping riverbank. It was carrying precious cargo — Saoirse coming for a holiday she'd earned back in St Alban's. Around the headland from Dartmouth, we caught up with Ollie and his crew, the sailing friends I'd come to learn from. We had a day together in Salcombe, then they sailed back to the Solent without me. I couldn't bring myself to leave. It was the water. Surely not British, seas of azure and cerulean lapping soft white beaches.

Saoirse and I anchored *Isean* for the first time, by Sunny Cove's arc of golden sand. A dream achieved, and another step in my education. 'But I would never be able to anchor overnight,' I told Saoirse. 'How can people sleep?' Some locals mentioned a beautiful spot, fifteen miles farther west. I was heading east, to prepare for the sail back to Portsmouth. 'Oh, it would be a shame to miss it,' they said. 'It's quite special.' People do this. It's fatal. We set sail. West. Three hours later, rounding a headland indented with white coves, we cruised in, where the charts indicated the mouth of the River Yealm. There were acres of rolling hills and low cliffs glowing rusty orange in the last rays of sun, sandbanks to port – children surreally cartwheeling in the sea. A hidden cove protected from swell. Glassy flat, dazzling emerald, carpeted by seagrass. There was one boat on anchor. A little Westerly – even smaller than *Isean*. It was *Little Mo*. And Debbie. We glided across, like planing into Oz. Delighted.

'I anchored for the first time today,' I called. 'Is it good holding?' Back came Debbie's wide smile, the customary reassurance, understated, feminine, supportive, as she assessed my little CQR anchor. 'It'll hold a treat here.' For the second time that day we let down the chain. Saoirse dived in the sunset; I paddled around on the dinghy. Debbie came over with mackerel. She'd caught so many, she said, she'd been sharing them with passing boats. Someone gave her a bottle of wine in return, someone else a book – fleeting friendships made fast on the water. We opened some wine, cooked the mackerel, spent the evening in this calm, still place, the sky ablaze, the fish jumping, talking of the life she lives at sea. I hadn't really considered such a thing – a community of people living and travelling off our coast, the kindly bartering, the slow pace and gentleness of it all. It seemed so simple, so accessible. I'd gone in the wrong direction that morning, but I knew, in that moment, that I was exactly where

I was supposed to be. I was happier than I could remember, swinging gently on anchor. And I slept like a baby.

A couple of days later, on a squally, foggy morning, I waved goodbye to Debbie and dropped Saoirse at Plymouth. I harnessed myself to *Isean* – safety first, I'd promised my dad – and sailed to the old fishing village of Polperro. It was just twenty miles away, but seemed farther, a journey that crossed a geographical and psychological border, from Devon to Cornwall, from reliance to independence. I'd gone on my own. I didn't acquit myself well on this first solo passage. I made slow progress, then mistakenly sailed into the inner harbour as it was fast drying out and only narrowly avoided the indignity of running aground. I sped back to deeper water and struggled to moor between two buoys, endlessly rowing back and forth, tying ropes together for length. Exhausted, I hauled myself back into the boat, intent on collapsing in a heap. But first, a quick check in the engine bay. The bilge was full of water, within inches of overflowing. Adrenaline provided all the energy I needed. I must have made quite an impression on the quiet families crabbing with buckets and spades. Such a pretty little boat in this most picturesque of harbours. An idyllic scene for visitors' sunset photographs. Then suddenly the most violent eruption of expletives, delivered in petrified Scottish, flowing across the water, and a startling string of missiles – berths, cushions, life jackets, fenders – forcefully ejected into the cockpit in my search for the manual bilge pump. At the peak of my panic, I finally remembered that I'd switched the automatic pump off, back in Salcombe. And I'd washed *Isean* down, filling her cockpit with water that had drained into the bilges – no wonder she'd been sluggish. What relief – for both her and me – when I turned the pump back on and an urgent stream came shooting out of the side.

By the time I dragged myself up to the Blue Peter pub, I

doubt there was a soul in the place who didn't know I was there. I wobbled my way to the bar where locals were cosily assembled, a window framing the scene nicely, and steadied myself on the counter with a twelve-thousand-yard stare, grasping for words. 'Wine,' I managed. 'White.' And for the avoidance of doubt, 'Big.' I sat outside on the sea wall, nursing the glass and staring at my girl as she bobbed peacefully in Cornwall's prettiest of harbours. I looked like a lunatic, and I felt like one too. But I'd done it. No more cajoling friends into being crew – I could do this myself. I had the freedom to sail when I wanted, when conditions were right, not when other people were free. A wonderful liberation. After that I couldn't turn back. I was set west for the summer, keeping *Isean* in Cornwall, travelling between her in my free time and London for work. At the end of the season, I found her a home on the Dart, the steam train chugging behind, fat seals snorting in front. And I went back to city life for the winter, but changed forever.

3

It was horribly busy in A&E. I was at London's University College Hospital with a headache that wouldn't quit. Two weeks earlier, I'd had a surfing lesson and the consensus was I had surfer's sinusitis, but the headaches were worsening and I was increasingly confused. I'd been to the GP twice and was mainlining painkillers and a nasal spray with steroids. A third visit to the doctor ended with the nurse on duty referring me for a precautionary brain scan, 'just to check'. Off I went on my scooter to Euston. The staff were run off their feet. It was 22 March 2017. I didn't know it, but the Westminster Bridge terrorist attack had just happened and all London hospitals were probably on standby. 'Why have they sent you here?' demanded a stressed-looking nurse, ushering me in to the doctor. Sheepishly, I passed my referral to him. 'I'm not going to read this,' he said. 'It will be wrong. You don't need a scan.' Taken aback, I was tempted to get out of there, but I repeated that I'd been feeling confused, getting a bit lost on my daily commute. Embarrassed, I added more detail. 'It's weird, I recognise people, but they look . . . different. And the keys to my scooter, they don't look like mine.' I realised it sounded daft. He went into a long diatribe about self-diagnosing online, his six-year training and Hippocrates, before instructing me to stand on one foot, arms out, touch my nose – all fine. 'I don't know why you're getting the weird recognition thing, but you don't need a scan,' he concluded. I felt uncertain, and guilty. I knew how badly under strain the NHS was – my mum had been a nurse – and I was horrified at the thought of being a time-waster. On the other hand, a nurse had recommended the scan and if I didn't have it, I'd be worried. He told me his staff were reluctant. 'They say, "Send her back to her GP."' Then he shifted to a conspiratorial tone. 'But I've been here for years. I can swing it for you.'

I was wheeled off and scanned, then I settled in for the wait, rejecting friends' offers of company. 'I'll be out soon.' I was wrong. A nurse called me in. 'Susan. Come in here. This is your bed.' My bed? I was confused – surely some mistake. 'Your head injury has been bleeding, and we're sending your scans to neurologists. When you hit your head . . .' I couldn't hear the rest with the blood rushing in my ears. 'Any questions?' I was dumbfounded. 'I . . . didn't hit my head,' I replied, slowly. 'Oh! You're the two-week headache?' 'YES!' I was almost shouting, adrenaline coursing through my body. 'Oh God, sorry. A similar case. Try not to panic.' She left. A tsunami of relief washed over me, a deep sympathy for whoever was receiving that terrifying news. Next, a surly doctor came in and demolished the relief. 'Right, you have a blood clot on the brain.' I could feel myself shrinking – I was just eyes, wide with disbelief. 'We're sending the scans to neurosurgeons.' I stared blankly. 'You look shocked,' he said. 'I thought I had sinusitis,' I managed, a voice so small it didn't sound like mine. He left and I dissolved into tears. Another nurse arrived and stroked my face. 'Susan, don't cry, you have to be strong now.' She added something about praying. 'We need to muster every bit of strength to fight this.' Holy shit, I thought, am I dying? I called Phil, who must have rung Saoirse, for she soon came skidding at breakneck speed around the corner, waving her hand in the air. 'I broke my thumb,' she announced grandly, then a pause. 'Maybe.' In her rush to the ward, two pints in, she'd crashed her bicycle. This cheered me enormously – business as usual – but when Phil turned up shortly afterwards, I was upset. I knew it was him, yet this man whose face I knew so well, he looked different. This 'weird recognition thing' had been happening for at least a week, but was almost imperceptible, and inconsistent. Some people looked the same; others looked subtly different, unfamiliar somehow. I'd felt silly telling the GPs. 'I'm not sure if I'm imagining this,' I'd start hesitantly. Once I knew what was causing it, I was terrified.

I was sure I hadn't hit my head. I'd gone to Lanzarote with my friend Cat. We'd had a surf lesson and I'd been knocked off my board several times. Three hours later, my energy was dropping and I was increasingly spaced out. I recall the sensation of cold little jabs starting on the top right-hand side of my head; by the time I reached the shore they had me moaning in pain. Sunstroke or dehydration, the instructor figured. I drank some water, wandered off, fell asleep in someone's garden, then found the hot, dusty main road where Cat was frantically looking for me. She bundled me to our holiday apartment, where I spent most of the remaining stay in bed. Back in London, I was straight to work at the *Guardian*, complaining about headaches, and with my inner compass ever so slightly out, getting a bit lost on the well-worn route home. It was so subtle, the cognitive change, just enough for me to doubt the ordinary things – keys, places, faces – that made up my world. I was in between knowing and not. Such an extraordinary thing, the cerebrum. Our own personal planet, that deep longitudinal fissure dividing left and right hemispheres. Trillions of synapses firing, billions of neurons transmitting, like stars in the Milky Way, too many to count. All that processing, thinking, knowing, feeling, remembering. All of it doing no less than defining us.

On some level, I had surely sensed a problem, yet I told myself it was fine, even if I was vague and uncertain, tired and emotional, quick to tears. That happens in life sometimes. I had known the consuming intensity of grief and its lingering sadness, the ordinary humdrum of romantic heartbreak, the anxiety of work stress or health scares – the stuff of life we each experience. I've been fortunate enough not to struggle with serious mental-health issues, but I'd had a tiny taste of how debilitating it must be a couple of years earlier. I'd suffered a spate of anxiety attacks, a sorrowful time. It came out of the blue, this grey. It could start with something as silly as lunchtime indecision in a sandwich shop. I'd pace back and forth until I left, with nothing but frustration, feel it build to anxiety and spiral into panic. Some days I'd wake with a jittery feeling and watch it descend to dread. Or I'd feel empty. There were short periods of feeling flat at best, dwelling on terrible losses ahead and the futility of trying to be happy; the afternoon I ran home from work to cry in bed. It was worse than grief in that there was no explanation, no knowing its nature or how to fix it. Was it stress? Diet? Too much caffeine or alcohol? Or the opposite – lacking in something, iron, B12? I tried cutting out stimulants, eating more greens and pulses. I sought deficiency-seeking blood tests – nothing obvious amiss. Just as the things that lift ordinary blues don't help with bone-deep sadness, I learned that what helped with grief was not effective for anxiety. When things felt bleak after Stephen's death, my mum would often drag us out for a walk, one foot in front of the other, feelings released to the sky instead of hanging heavy in the kitchen air. But getting out didn't help with the panic, and I couldn't find the will to do it anyway. I went to the sea, to *Isean*, and still I didn't feel joy. That was scarier than navigating any tidal race. On the other hand, I felt a return to myself cycling along the Brixton Road amid car horns and buses, bad-tempered shouting and pollution. And it was all beautiful. How grateful you are when the colours come back. I felt a deeper gratitude too. It is a gift, really, to experience the wide range of human emotions, to better connect when friends are struggling, to hear with more empathy. I learned to appreciate the beautiful mundanity of the everyday. I already knew how to love the small things – clean sheets, my cat snoring – and now I could appreciate even less. The absence of something, like the relief when physical pain goes. I observed the lifting of that heavy mood as a kind of miracle, the return of normal lightness, of feeling like myself. It didn't disappear overnight. I was plagued for a few miserable months before that palette of greys went off on its merry way. The relief of their disappearance was partially clouded by the lack of explanation, the fear of a return. It's strange how little we know about the mind. For the first time, I really understood how vulnerable we all are when it comes to something as fluid as mental well-being. I hadn't realised that something like this could creep up on me, that, seemingly out of nowhere, I'd feel so helplessly out of kilter. Like a tragedy hitting a family, these are not things that happen to other people. You learn – really learn – not to take happiness for granted, like expecting sunshine every day. Better embrace the changing seasons, the anticipation of what you've missed, holding a loved one, breaking a fast. That most welcome of things – the calm after the storm. When you're in the middle of your own little storm, though, you don't see so clearly.

Back in London, I had been trying to outrun mine, charging around town on my scooter, my cognitive compass awry. I'd be upset that a colleague looked different, then someone would mention they'd had a haircut. Good, I'd think, grasping that life raft; besides, I reasoned, pain causes stress and confusion. But it was becoming clear that things were not right. The headache developed into what I imagine a full-blown migraine feels like. I couldn't bear light, each step was agony. Once admitted, I spent two days in A&E. With friends, I awaited news from another duty doctor. He was a surfer, and while others surmised I had simply forgotten a blow to my head, he had a respect for the terrible power of waves and theorised that the force of the water could have created a whiplash effect. He also confirmed there was pressure on the part of my brain that controlled recognition. Aha! A hard fact that explained the distortion of something so subtle, so fundamental to my personality. Eventually, the surfer doctor brought good news – it was probably a small bleed that would naturally reabsorb – but he delivered it as though he was on a Spanish soap opera.

'We've looked again at the scans.'
Deafening silence.
'Am I worried?'
Stares off into the middle distance while executing the
   world's longest pause.
'No.'

But things changed again. The scans were inconclusive. I might have a very serious brain infection. I would need an MRI. Cat arrived as I headed off for it. Cat. One of my closest friends. Who says a soulmate has to be romantic? I have several. Life partners come in all forms, and friendships are often the most enduring. These are love stories too, free of surging and waning passions, the insecurities that can plague romances. Cat is someone who instinctively knows what's good for me and how to gently steer me towards it – a quality I cherished in my mum. She's the person you'd most want in a crisis. We met in 2014, after I was on a freelance assignment for the *Guardian*, writing about sea nomads in Thailand. I saw her work before I saw her: gorgeous intimate photographs she'd captured of the Moken people, the last of their kind to live at sea. Cat Vinton. Even her name was cool. I was bowled over by her talent and wondered where in the world this enigmatic woman lived. I was in Bangkok airport when I located her on a boat on London's Regent's

Canal! And yes, she'd love to meet up. A few days later, there she was, grinning at me on a cold morning in Haggerston. Dark glossy hair, clear green eyes, tanned and slim, as warm as the stove glowing in her narrowboat. Our friendship was instantaneous, the bond strong from the start. Her photography and my writing made us natural collaborators. We'd take off on freelance assignments, usually in pursuit of sea-based tales, to Thailand, Myanmar, Mexico, travels packed full of hair-raising incidents. Now she was in the ward; worried, of course, but with the kind of optimism and strength that filled the room, the kind you need.

I was feeling glum at the MRI, it's fair to say, the needle for contrast dye lodged uncomfortably in my hand, when I met a lovely young guy. He thought he'd seen me in the cancer unit. 'No,' I said, registering the seriousness of his condition. 'Not yet?' he asked. I smiled sadly, sifting through my mess of feelings – fear, hope, sympathy – looking for an appropriate response, and asked about him instead. He lived by the sea, in Chichester. Beautiful. I told him I'd sailed there and he remembered – he'd once lived on a boat near me in London. He'd had a little boy since then. 'You've got to be positive,' he said, smiling. He was right, of course. The encounter ought to have given me perspective about my relative good fortune, but instead I was left with foreboding for myself, and sadness for the gravity of what he faced. I'd seen this kind of understated strength before. Anyone who has lost people they love to disease has been humbled by it. Not long before my mum died, we lost my cousin Lorraine to cancer. She was like an older sister to me; we'd grown up together and I loved her dearly. I trailed after her from childhood into adolescence. As we grew, she indulged my childish games and I watched wide-eyed as nervous boys approached to ask her out. She was always laughing, sparky, feminine; her arms jangling with those cheap eighties bangles, metallic blue, silver, green. She had a natural beauty that didn't need adornment; it radiated all the way from childhood to 2003, aged thirty-four, far too young to be in that Glasgow ward. I'd had the privilege of staying with her, the two of us in her hospital room on a May night that was one of her last, her baby, Lucy, just months old at home. In the early morning as she slept, I heard the door open and my mum quietly slipped in with us. A vibrant scarf defying her hair loss, a smile so full of love, of strength, resilience, compassion, so knowing. My mum had just under a year left. The enormity of that. The three of us, simply there together in the peace of the early morning. The dawn light and the scent of flowers. Love, pure and simple, unspoken and understood. The courage and dignity of it. That will stay with me forever. I left Lorraine, knowing I'd never see her again, grateful for that night, for the old familiarity and love, the laugh as we woke to my phone alarm, the easy friendship that lasted all the way.

Back to the ward after my scan, I found myself once again in the strong embrace of female friendship. Cat, her enormous smile lighting up that grim room, making it all bearable. A couple of hours later, the surfer doctor returned. 'Good news,' he grinned. 'It's not infected. It's a mini-bleed which is reabsorbing. It should heal itself. You can go home.' I was one of the lucky ones after all. Relief flooded, then elation, just before the exhaustion that would hit at home. I was giddily chatty as Cat and I left the hospital. I wondered where my scooter was parked. No, surely I wouldn't need a cab. I never get a cab. On I chatted, telling Cat how I'd almost drowned as a child on a little polystyrene surfboard in Perranporth in Cornwall. I remember seeing this huge wave and instead of going over it, I'd gone through it, then down. I'd always thought Stephen had rescued me, the big brother I'd cast forever as hero, but memory is unreliable – it was he who had pushed me off and my dad who had run into the sea to pluck me out, limp in my little blue swimsuit. My dad! I hadn't told him I was in hospital. I didn't want to worry him. I'd tell him now that I was okay. 'Anyway,' I rambled on as Cat hugged me goodbye, 'surfing's just not my sport.' She firmly pushed me into a cab home. 'Sailing, though . . .'

And my inner compass was pointing straight in that direction. After the summer with *Isean*, and inspired by Debbie's example, I wanted more. I had just applied for and accepted voluntary redundancy from my job of thirteen years – while suffering a mini-brain haemorrhage. I'd taken the decision to quit in Lanzarote. Cat and I sat with a coffee as I held my aching head. 'Do you know what? I'm ready,' I'd said. She'd known immediately what I meant, had quietly encouraged it. Whenever we'd travelled, I'd been reluctant to return to office life, and she'd seen me flourish on *Isean*, happy at sea with the dolphins and the seals. The offer of redundancy had come up a few times over the years – the inexorable decline in newspaper sales meant it kept rearing its head – but I had never been able to imagine leaving my job at the *Guardian*, just as I could never have imagined getting a job at the *Guardian*. I'd spent my first years in London working in a bank, before belatedly starting university at twenty-four, then a job in the arts in Brighton. In my early thirties, I got around to pursuing a media career. It was something I'd dreamed of as a child, illustrated by the pencil-and-crayon magazines I filled with adventure and tragedy. Here, the fantastical world of talking mermaids; there, the imaginary news report of little 'Hugh Black', lost at sea, staring sadly off the page in his NHS glasses. As an adult, I was less prolific, dismissed journalism as too competitive. In Brighton Marina I met Jeff Howlett – a sailor, jazz musician and ex-hack who taught media. I loved him right away – warm hands, bare feet, big grin. He taught me to sail. And then he taught me journalism. Jeff is the kind of person you should look out for in life – or even better, try to be – all encouragement, taking the mystery out of things. 'Journalism is no black art,' he'd told me. It was a trade. You just had to work hard. My confidence boosted, I completed the NCTJ, then blagged my way into the *Guardian*, the paper I'd bought since my late teens and the only place I ever wanted to work. I remember Stephen's teasing as he spotted me with it. 'You like the idea,' he'd laugh. 'Intend to read the serious stuff, then flick through to the features section.' He knew, he said, because he did the same. He would have approved of how I ended up there – I'd called on the off-chance and reached a stressed editor left suddenly short-handed on the subbing desk. 'Oh yeah, I've got experience,' I lied. I turned up, terrified, but somehow it paid off. After a few years of hard work, I landed an editing job, largely providing entertaining features to help balance out the paper's more serious coverage. By definition, it was the most fun imaginable.

I had achieved more than I thought possible – security, a good income, a job that felt more like messing around with mates than a proper career. But the thing no one tells you when you're young is not that you can achieve your dreams. It is the extraordinary fact that you outgrow them. The pace of work life is so fast that we tend not to mark achievements – a promotion, the completion of a project, a new job. We have a drink to celebrate, then move on to the next challenge, the next stressful deadline, the next bill, the next worry. We revise our expectations up, forget our previous selves who would have been amazed at the accomplishments. Always, we're thinking about what we can't yet do. How often I'd reminded myself that I'd done better than I ever imagined – my younger self would have been blown away. So why am I not happier? I should be grateful. It's all I ever wanted. When you're telling yourself, all the time, that you should be happy, you know it's no longer working. In order to keep growing, we need new dreams. Mine had changed. My weekends were spent with *Isean* on the Dart, and on each return to London, the happier part of me was still floating with her. I was unbound – drifting, like flotsam in the grand old Thames, steadily, inevitably straight out to sea. For the first time, I could imagine a better alternative to the life I had. I sat there in Lanzarote with my weird headache and said it out loud. Then I went home and started the process – evidently brain-injury me was really decisive and dynamic.

After my brief hospital stay, I had just a couple of months left in employment, most of which was spent recovering. I was fragile. Colleagues and friends rallied, bringing food, flowers and love. It was a gentle time on the old wooden boat I lived on in London. I'd been there for over ten years. Phil and I had moved life and home from Brighton to the capital in 2004, the year we lost my mum. We had the boat but no experience; we hired a professional skipper and my dad came along for the trip. Left along the coast – Dover, North Foreland and the Isle of Sheppey – up into the mercurial mouth of the Thames. We were welcomed into the city by a porpoise, a dark fin rolling through silver waves. I could feel my mum's smile at the strange poetry of that. We followed the bends and curves, where the river loops wide around the Isle of Dogs, past the Thames sailing barges that still drift, as in T. S. Eliot's *The Waste Land*, down Greenwich Reach. '*With the turning tide / Red sails / Wide / To leeward, swing on the heavy spar.*' On we went, past the meridian line, two miles from a new life in Deptford. My dad and I looked to port as we passed Maritime Greenwich, and there she was. The *Cutty Sark*, her three masts rising gracefully, 150 feet into the London sky. I had found my place beside this old friend from Dumbarton. It was the best way to live in the capital, on this mighty river, flooding in from the North Sea. There's magic there too. Thousands of seals make a living in the city; sea horses and sharks breed in the estuary; whales visit more often than you'd know. For years I crossed the Thames on my way to work, scanning the surface, hoping for a glimpse of something. I was in love with the life I had built there, with the job, the people, the city. Which was the best way to leave it.

Now I was setting off without a plan. But the amorphous nature of that appealed. I'm not one of life's planners, not someone who loudly sets goals. It came from my mum, who didn't like to set up grand expectations. I'd rather quietly do things than talk about doing them and perhaps fail. I spoke simply of sailing into the sunset. The response from friends and colleagues was often the same. 'Amazing,' they'd say, glassy-eyed, trying to imagine such a thing. 'What then?' I didn't know what then. People were baffled at the lack of purpose, confused by the vagueness in my replies about sailing for as long as I could make the money stretch. I hadn't put a time limit on my trip – it wasn't a year or two out. I wasn't going off on some challenge or to prove anything. It was far gentler than that, but much bigger too. I was seeking nothing less than a completely different life. I understood why it frightened people. It did me too – it had taken years to find the courage to leave. It was scary to give up my income, but it was more than that. My job was a big part of me. I was proud of it. It had taken a lot of work to get and I was giving up something I'd never get back. In leaving, my identity was altered. In a world where we all go around trying to get a handle on each other, where 'what do you do?' is shorthand for 'what sort of person are you?', I was now someone without a job at all. I was just myself. But that's enough, isn't it? When I think about the people I love most in the world, what they are paid to do is the least interesting thing about them. Seeing Debbie's choices had reinforced that. I was full of admiration for her courage to follow her desires. I wanted to do the same. The ego can be difficult to manage, though, especially after years of competing in a career-driven society. Questions of identity can throw you into existential crisis, threaten to scare you off course. *What am I? Who am I?* It's about holding your nerve through these wobbles. Facing emotional panic is a bit like unsettled weather: you do what you need, set the storm sail and keep calm. It's a skill I would learn on the journey. In the meantime, if I needed a label, if I was insecure enough to need affirmation, to validate my choice, it was simple. I was now a sailor.

I was also wise enough to reconsider after my injury. I wasn't overly concerned about my mental state – it made sense that I was emotionally fragile after a brain haemorrhage. I had known far worse. But I would have to be strong, physically and mentally, before I actually set off. I never doubted it. If I'd learned one thing through the hospital trauma, as with the other mini-traumas in life, it was the importance of grasping every bit of joy while you can. Doing what you love, not delaying it, not dreaming about a future when you will be ready to do it. Doing it. Doing it now. If I'd had any second thoughts, they were obliterated on the first Monday morning after I quit. I went out for a cycle, newly liberated and full of excitement. I stopped and looked down at the Thames. There it was. Just below me. Unmistakable. A seal. Right beside the ferry terminal I'd passed every day for ten years. One day of freedom and already my eyes knew how to look.

4.

Big fat wet drops of rain pelted the deck, rivulets coursed down *Isean*'s windows. Torrential. Dartmouth was a waterworld, its streets now streams, its people hunched forward, wading through the driving downpour. The dinghy, floating alongside us on the river, had filled up – that would need bailing again. It kept coming, cascading over *Isean* in heavy sheets, a waterfall. She loves fresh water spilling fast and hard through all the crevices, clearing out the salt and grit, dirt and debris – a good body scrub. Let it rain! And let it rain properly – better these heavy downpours than a drab, clammy British drizzle that coats the dirt in damp without shifting it, like your aunt's spittle-soaked hankie wiping the muck around your face in a drying slick.

A caravan roof or a boat deck is the perfect amplifier for this particular din. You hear it before you see it: the tell-tale pitter-patter, like birds' feet – 'is that rain?' – then steadier, heavier, until it's streaming down the windows, blurring everything outside your own little world. It invites lazy afternoons and introspection, tea and comfort and a good book, nostalgia for childhood holidays. Many of those I spent with my mum, cousin Lorraine and our gran – Maw Joss – at a caravan in Newdale, a midge-infested campsite near my aunt Eileen's house on the Isle of Mull. It rains a lot in the Western Isles. Hammering hailstones or black ice, Maw Joss sent us out in it. Any hesitance would elicit scorn. 'Away wae ye,' she'd spit in a heavy Irish brogue, her eyes narrowing in contempt at the perceived drama – what fussy wean won't play in thunderstorms? 'Liz Taylor's only running efter her,' she'd complain of me. Maybe she had a point: I knew how to play the tragic heroine. On the way home from school sometimes I'd slow down by roadside puddles as cars approached, pathetic and helpless as the sheet of icy water cascaded over me. When I appeared suitably drenched at the back door, my mum would make a big, warm fuss of me – all tea and sympathy, hot towels and love. Maw Joss didn't work like that; she liked us tough. My dad found Lorraine and me one morning, asleep like a pair of Egyptian mummies, half standing, half slumped against the wall inside her garden hut. 'Surely,' he checked with her, 'they're not sleeping there overnight?' 'Acht!' she would have hissed in incredulous denial. But my memories are of knocking on her front window at night to tell her 'That's us home,' then heading to the hut or back to the park. Wildly inappropriate overnight accommodation for children. But character-building, inuring us to frosty Scottish nights and midges in the morning. Something for me to draw on in this, my first week of freedom. It was early June 2017 and I had quit my job in order to sail around Britain in one of the worst summers in living memory.

I'd joined *Isean* where she was tied to Barry's bright-yellow yacht-rigging barge on the Dart. He'd replaced most of her shrouds and stays ('vintage' he'd politely called them), and she looked amazing, with her winter paint job glimmering through the rain. I had spent my savings, final wages and a good chunk of the redundancy money on safety – new rigging, radio, personal locator beacon, safety lines, waterproof torches – an endless list adding up to many thousands of pounds. Not a fan of spreadsheets, I hadn't set a detailed budget. It was rough and loose: fifteen pounds a day for mooring costs, the same for food and the same again as contingency. If that worked, it would stretch for a couple of years and I could top it up with earnings here and there – freelance writing and editing, pub work if necessary. I would set off west, to Land's End, then turn north.

I'd sail round the UK slowly, seeing this island and its people from the sea. If I considered the whole trip in one go, it sounded intimidating, but I now knew that any long trip is just a series of smaller trips. It would mostly be a bunch of day sails, like I'd already done. I'd take my time, avoid bad weather, seek shelter in marinas and help from friends on the way. See how far I got before the weather turned, then decide what to do. It wasn't much of a plan, but it was a direction. We spent our first wet week on the Dart. *Isean* didn't leave the side of her cheery yellow companion, while I thrashed the oars against the tide upriver. I floated in the dinghy in a downpour surrounded by trees full of water and life, the thick wooded banks agleam. I discovered my sailing waterproofs were no longer waterproof, my bum itchy with damp, my socks sucking rainwater through my leaky old boots. Back home drenched, and my mum not there to dry me off. But if there's one thing she taught me, it was how to take care of myself, how to be happy. Her outlook was always set towards the positive, what you had rather than what you didn't. I had tea. I had towels. And I had *Isean*.

The storms finally abated and we headed west to the Kingsbridge Estuary. This deep inlet, like the beautiful rias of northern Spain, is actually a drowned river valley. I stopped in a bucolic spot that felt more farmyard than sea, waking to bleating sheep and bellowing bulls. I rowed up to the little market town, all pretty narrow alleys – Squeezebelly Lane – and cobbled streets. I was excited to be on a rare outing to a restaurant, Wild Artichokes, run by my friend, the gifted cook Jane Baxter. Ushered in to join locals on one of the communal tables, I met people who had been on a mission to rescue a humpback whale trapped in fishing net, so I found much to like about the company. Around midnight, tipsy and stuffed with croquettes and sage butter, I tumbled, heavy as pig-iron ballast, into my poor dinghy as it sighed and sank a little in protest. Three miles to *Isean* and bed: I slipped out into the silent night, bracing myself for a tiring ride home. Almost immediately, the journey turned magical, the sea as still as a millpond and effortless to row, a sky bursting with constellations. I lowered my gaze, my eyes drawn by water as starry as above. It twinkled and sparkled with bioluminescence; a following wake of glowing foam melted the miles away. With each dip of the oars, more starbursts exploded. I dreamed my way home, gliding on a silver river, stars below and above, like flying through a galaxy.

What did it matter if it took time? Time was now expansive. Hours stretched idly as *Isean* and I meandered our way west on days long with summer light. We proceeded at walking pace, a tempo that alters your focus. I'd never noticed how special gannets are, so different from gulls. Gleaming white, their black-tipped wings so striking, their flight so graceful, the power of that elongated dive. There was so much detail to notice – with time, with eyes wide open. The stress and stuff of land drifted into the background, of no use out here. My inner clock, perpetually ticking through twenty-five years of a working life – sleep, work, eat, spend, work, rest, work – was altered. My pendulum was now swinging to the rhythms of the natural world, my daily routine dependent on the weather. My needs were fundamental – where will I get water, food, shelter? The days would finish when we arrived and that would depend on the wind, the swell, the tides – the wax and wane of the moon. They'd start differently too. Sometimes I'd wake up and enjoy a lazy day; sometimes I'd rise and raise the sails before putting the kettle on, with weather or sea conditions – or the prospect of a long slog – dictating my moves. As I discovered quickly, the best feeling in the world was when I'd dispensed with the land-based chores – stocked up with food, water, fuel – and found shelter to relax and explore. I was now feeling brave enough to venture out of harbours and marinas to anchor at sea, opening up wonderful possibilities. With each bit of progress and learning, I was buying independence.

So it was that the dinghy came into its own in the unexpected beauty of Plymouth's backwaters. We sailed up the Tamar, the handsome river that forms the boundary between Devon and Cornwall. We found our way into the Lynher, a tributary branching west and winding through Cornish granite, slate and clay up to peaty Bodmin Moor. *Isean* and I took the rising tide upriver to the quiet little anchorage of Dandy Hole. It's a well-named place, a reassuringly deep pool that offers a minimum depth of three metres when the water around runs shallow with the falling tide. It was well sheltered too, judging by a couple of hulking old boats that looked like they'd been there forever, held steadfast on their anchors. It is where I really learned how to anchor. I'd never felt confident, always worrying that we'd drag. In the peace of Dandy Hole, I tested the theory. I'd underestimated our swinging circle – the radius that wind and tide shift us round – and I hadn't been digging the anchor in hard enough. I practised going full-throttle reverse until I was sure we were firmly embedded. There is more than a little comfort in knowing you're safely fixed to a point in the seabed. Held fast, still moving, flexible, yet grounded. It's an anchoring of the senses too, and a freedom you've earned, to be safely at home in a world made of magic, on shimmering seas.

I had a peaceful and happy time learning under a full moon, trout leaping from the water around me. Finally, confident that *Isean*'s anchor was set, I braved our first separation in the wild, leaving her in idyllic surroundings while I went off by dinghy to explore. Another kind of freedom bought by confidence in my anchor. I visited St Germans, a pretty little hamlet. Not far from there, as the water ebbed, I found an enchanted crescent of ivory beach, a momentary gift uncovered by the tides. My feet sank into virgin sands that would soon vanish, an ephemeral world that belonged to sea creatures but for a short time was mine. I floated the hours away, watched as the beach was returned to the crabs and the fish. I followed the tide as it flooded in, up into little creeks and streams that narrowed and shallowed until they were barely there. A half-and-half world where I bumped the dinghy over mud, unable to distinguish river from land. I found forgotten bridges and disused tunnels, hidden watery passageways overgrown and wild. I drifted under low-hanging trees, lost in freedom and birdsong in the afternoon sun, and I couldn't really believe my luck. So recently liberated, I had to keep reminding myself that this was my life now, that no one could take it from me. It's a superstition that remains from life-changing news straight out of the sky. Joy must be treasured, for it can be taken in a moment. There was a more mundane fear too, of a return to the other life I'd made, the one with obligations and bills and daily commutes. I didn't want that life back. I had to reassure myself that this life I was living now was the real one. No phone call could come that would haul me back into an office. There was no returning to weeks filled with emails and meetings. I was here with the gannets, seals and crabs, and it was all fine.

Eventually I headed to *Isean* – the thought bringing more joy, turning the river bend to where I would find her, that first glimpse of the mast pulling my mouth into a smile. I arrived home. The dinghy full of leaves and branches, me studded with twigs and covered in mud. A mess, the pair of us, trailing river clay all over *Isean*'s gunwales and deck. I thought I heard her sigh as she took us in. In these still moments I appreciated her quiet sanctuary as much as her strength in rough seas. My heart swelled with gratitude – that she had brought me to this special place, that she was there, as always, waiting to welcome me. I rinsed the mud from my feet, cooked a simple dinner and collapsed on my berth in a rush of happy exhaustion, an outdoorsy tired from a day spent on nothing but adventuring. I was completely at one with my surroundings, a thing in nature; my skin salty from the sea, my hair a tangled mess, turning blonde from the sun. I felt a snug, warm glow, reminiscent of childhood, I suppose, but with the agency of adulthood. I was rocked to sleep in an instant in the sanctum of *Isean*'s maternal hull.

Once before, as an adult, I had found myself in that kind of childlike state, a place of feeling not thinking, where everything was simple. It was at my mum's funeral – the celebration, really, of her life. My last days with her had been full of privilege. It was quiet and peaceful. But when she left us, I was not silent. My pain rushed out in an animal cry, something physical about the knowledge, my body screaming that she was gone. In the days and weeks that followed, an extraordinary calm came. I felt held. I didn't fall apart. She had achieved the impossible. She had taken the blackness out of death. She had lightened it, as if it didn't have to be such a heavy dark void. This was my mum's enduring gift – light in the dark. We had a party in her style. Her friend Christine had the keys to a church in the Gorbals in Glasgow and we had the run of it. We arrived hours before the service, music blasting as we decorated. Colourful balloons, I remember, and a huge Buddha we brought. Tibetan prayer flags fluttering amongst the crosses. Everything jumbled together. I watched as mourners filed in for the service, a grave-looking line of people, faces white, many in black. 'They look so sad,' I remember thinking, floating up there in my own little world – as if they were the abnormal ones. We had been lucky in being there early. I felt comfortable, as if we were welcoming everyone into our home. My mum would love that. Colours draped everywhere; none of the heavy, nervous formality that surely makes everyone feel worse. My brother David played accordion as everyone arrived; a friend, Jim Daly, played the

Irish pipes. My cousins read beautiful words: Henry Van Dyke's ship, her mast and spars, white sails spreading to the blue ocean. My mum always encouraged me to sing in public, but I never would until that day. With Christine, I sang for her. 'Like a bird,' the words soared, 'from these prison walls I'll fly,' and it came so naturally, this birdsong rising up and out of me. When we left, the church was full of laughter. We were open to my mum's kind of joy as well as our own sadness, celebrating her love of the left-field.

We had planned a woodland burial and organised who would carry her wicker coffin to the place we had chosen. An oak tree would be planted. I had decided not to be one of those bearers – she wasn't there any more, I thought. I didn't need to do it. The day felt as if it would be for other people; I'd rather have a private goodbye. Perhaps I'd find it an ordeal. I wouldn't have the strength. I had misjudged myself. When the time came to carry my mum, I found I was standing up. I wanted to take her those last steps. I replaced my cousin Conrad; quietly, in kindness, he gave way. I had no idea how special the ceremony would be, how important those last moments were. That the ritual would run so deep it would become a part of me. To honour her body as well as her soul; to carry her, carefully and respectfully; to gently lay her, with all the love I've ever known, into the earth. By the graveside, our friend Neily played the fiddle. I cried. And I stopped crying. I was completely unselfconscious, my mum's little girl again. I remember being there in a bright dress, no shoes, running around with an unexpected and sudden openness that felt so natural. Full of love. And it was for everyone, friends and strangers, old rivals and foes; there was simply no room for other feelings.

I was operating at a different level, as we can in times of grief. A different experience from the overwhelming shock and despair of Stephen's funeral almost a decade earlier. But even those dark days brought forth the extraordinary, the chance to rise above the fray, to see and feel love, pure and unadulterated. As painful as they were, I valued those times for the perspective and emotional clarity they brought, the focus on what matters – and what really doesn't. For the melting away of everyday nonsense. The visceral nature of a family thrown together, raw with feelings. I cherished those times for the space they allowed me to inhabit, the self-awareness and connection to others. Like a version of myself that is honest and true, calm and kind, not plagued by insecurities and petty doubts. It's like flying up above it all, as close as I know to true compassion, love that's unconditional. I always wondered if it was possible to reach that place without the pain of loss preceding it. Perhaps, in nature, in time, I was finding a way there.

It was time to leave my little sanctuary and rejoin society. Just a couple of miles, a gentle curve to port, and there it all was – the bustle and noise of the world, the busy Tamar. The river runs wide and deep here, but I was heading just over eight miles north, where it narrows through the undulating Tamar Valley. You need the rising tide to round the bends and curves to Calstock. I was apprehensive about *Isean*'s keel – once the tide leaves, there's not enough water to get back downriver. But I could see the little pools of reassuring white on the charts too. Another dandy hole. *Isean* would be safe, deep in the country, sitting in her own personal well. How splendidly surreal. Courage, I whispered, as we set off, venturing deep inland, nearer Dartmoor's national park than open sea. We put-putted our way up using the tide and the little Yanmar 9 h.p. engine. It was a calm, still day and I was soon enjoying this chocolatey-brown river, the novelty of cutting through thick Cornish and Devonshire woodland and flowery banks. The countryside! A patchwork of luminous grassy fields, forests and meadows, like a Battenberg cake divided by hedges rustling with wings.

Amid it all, ghosts linger from another age – the atmospheric old tin mines, their ruined towers and engine houses, discarded shells around the valleys and woodlands. At the height of the boom a hundred mines lined this river, supplying much of the world's copper and tin. If you close your eyes you can imagine the noise. If I closed my eyes, I'd end up stuck in the mud, so I didn't try.

The first thing that greets your arrival in Calstock is the Edwardian viaduct, its graceful arches mirrored in the quiet flow of the river below. Just before it, a historic boatyard, and beyond it, a small quay squatted by a flock of unlovely Muscovy ducks, all red-faced and wheezily hissing. The village is incredibly pretty – Victorians once visited in paddle steamers, and tourists still come by boat from Plymouth – but it has a pleasingly lived-in feel, young working families enjoying the beauty of their environment. One of those families was there to greet me – my friends, transplanted from London days, Tom and Fleur and their kids I hadn't yet met. I was pleased to make a good first impression. I was wielding a freshly caught mullet and regaled the girls with the tale of how I'd unexpectedly hooked it that morning, still in my underwear. Unprepared as it thrashed around my cockpit, I'd dispatched it in a panic with the closest thing I had to hand – the case of a forty-piece socket set, covering myself in fish scales in the process. We all set off back to their house to gut it, three-year-old Lilla and five-year-old Etta soon also happily covered in fish innards while their baby brother Felix looked on wide-eyed. This new life of mine allowed time for bonding. We walked through fields shining with glow-worms. I taught them about the boat, Etta's little face a study of concentration as she learned how to helm. I attended school sports day. The smell of cut grass and parents cheering and ribbons – a sweet family experience I would not ordinarily have had. I love to see the different paths friends and family have taken, lives full of love and nature, houses and gardens, pets and community. Happy lives I could imagine inhabiting. I always return to my own life enriched and embrace the choice I've made all over again. There are so many good ways to live.

I don't have children. I think I'd be good at it, but I was never able to work out if it was something I wanted. I'd had no big urges either way, no fantasies of marriage and kids when I was growing up, no longing, no physical ache. There was a distinct absence of pressure on me in this regard, as in so many other things. When I was in long-term relationships, I didn't have to endure the weight of wondering – 'Will there be grand-children?' – from my parents. My mum fiercely guarded my autonomy and was appalled by that kind of prying. Even though I didn't know whether I'd have kids – hadn't thought about it – perhaps she knew, in the way that mothers know their children. We had conversations on the subject. She'd wondered what her life might have been like without us. 'Travelling,' she said, a wistful look in her eye. She must have known the sort of person I'd become – that I essentially already was – even though I didn't yet know myself. There were plenty of ways for a woman to live her life, she was saying; motherhood isn't the pinnacle. She was cheering me on, whatever I chose to do. Later in life, when I did think about children, I found there was quite a lot I didn't fancy about having them, from the personal (the loss of freedom, the responsibility and worry – forever) to the more existential (we already number too many) and the irrational (the absolute certainty that I would spend the full nine months terrified of labour). On the other side of that was potential regret. In the end, I decided that if I'd wanted children, I'd have done something about it. My ambivalence was the answer I needed, and I trusted that nature wouldn't burden me with a cruel desire my body couldn't meet.

I love the young people I have in my life, the open conversations that take such unexpected turns. We forget that children are wise. I admire how they interrogate everything, questioning how stuff works. I don't know when we lose that, when we become afraid to admit that we don't know things, but it's a great shame we do. We often talk of childlike qualities as weaknesses. Too much emotion is unsophisticated. Too much honesty is undiplomatic. Talk of fairness is childish idealism, too simplistic. But sometimes things are simple. Sometimes we complicate things to feel more adept; make complex systems that don't work. These days on the planet, it feels like children are the adults in the room. I love how brutally honest children are, how imaginative and fearless they can be, how open their hearts are, their keen sense of justice. How they don't waste time on stuff they're not interested in, and – perhaps most of all – how naturally and fully they live in the moment. This was something I was starting to recapture myself. Perhaps that connects me to the children of family and friends. It's my favourite thing when children take to me, like a vote of confidence. They haven't developed the shells and masks we hide behind, so they tend to see past ours, straight to the heart of us. I'll forever remember one of my favourite aunts, my dad's sister Margaret. She was fiercely intelligent, a woman who would stay up all night debating politics. People found her intimidating. But to me she was the opposite. I loved her passion, felt her deep kindness and, my God, she was so stimulating. She always took the time to discuss things with me, from politics to her spiritual beliefs, was full of praise and encouragement, never treated me like a kid. Her attention felt like such a compliment, and it gave me confidence. I thrived, as though her very interest in me made me more interesting. When you meet people like that, you don't forget them. Maybe we're all that way to someone. At the very least, I hope I don't patronise the children I know. I have an advantage. It must stick in their minds, this strange adult turning up in a little boat like a character blown in from adventure on the high seas. I think it inspires kids – still so open in their thinking – to know there are all these impossibly unusual ways to live. It's particularly pleasing if I can inspire kids, because the older I get, the more they inspire me.

5

Back to sea. Off to the end of land, away from the pastoral, the pretty order of serene lawns, blackbirds and cottages, farms and ploughed earth. The tide carried us back down the sheltered rivers of the Tamar Valley, a gentle shove – like your brother teaching you to ride a bicycle – and we were out. Back to the westerly winds and Atlantic swell, a sea that demands your full attention, enthusiastic waves rising up in greeting. And what a show. The full palette of blues – navy, indigo, denim, azure – a cloudless sky of lunchtime cobalt scattered on diamond shards of water. Back to the excitement of squawking gulls chasing fishing boats, common dolphins chasing *Isean*. The sweet smell, like melon wrapped up in salt. My hand trailing in the water, the cold spray salting my bird's-nest hair, shocking my face into laughter. Such joy. West again. Sailing again. Up with the main, out with the jib, a strong breeze bending it into its elegant curve. The engine off on a well-earned break, and peace from its steady rattle and throb. Instead, the whoosh and hiss of the hull cutting through water and the familiar creaking, like the sound of a loved one's gait, just so, on the landing. *Isean* coming to life, adjusting herself into position, a little squeak here, a little sigh there, like stretching old muscles, everything falling into place. Speeding up, she takes off. 'You're cycling yourself,' your brother shouts from a distance; he let go.

I was in my element: *Isean* and I, back in the rhythm of the sea – a heady mix of comfort and adventure that would never get old. We stopped in St Mawes, near Falmouth, my first experience of anchoring in a storm. The wind was gale force – a good test. Out in the cockpit in the driving wind and rain, I was apprehensive, anxiously checking position as lightning forked and skies darkened. I stared at the markers on land – 'Are they moving? Are we moving?' Slowly, others emerged too, hooded figures braced against the blow, out for a look as we were each thrown around. A man on the neighbouring yacht raised his drink, a simple gesture that gave me a lift. We were all in it together. The harbour master came by in his speedboat after the worst of it, gave me a thumbs-up. These little moments of human connection – how special they are. Feeling bonded to others, grateful for their presence, the solidarity of a little wave. While it's of comfort, though, the reality is that you're usually alone dealing with things going wrong in bad conditions; the same strong gust that caused your anchor to drag has broken someone else's line – everyone has to look after their own boats in a crisis. We were fine in this, our first little squall outside a harbour, but the following weeks' forecasts were not bringing cheer. I was preoccupied with weather for good reason – ahead of me, the Lizard peninsula, jutting right out into the Channel, marks the most southerly point in mainland Britain. Guarded by not one but two lighthouses, warning of turbulent and rock-strewn waters, it's now a mecca for wreck divers. Always a bad sign. And after that, Land's End.

Cornwall is at its wildest and most remote where the land runs out to its end. In sharp contrast to the theme park marking the landmark above, this coast is naturally dramatic. South of the headland, Wolf Rock lighthouse howls as strong winds rush through the fissures in its base. Farther north, the Longships lighthouse, evoked on Turner's canvas in a half-seen terror of furious sea and splintered ship. It feels more like realism than romanticism in this place of monstrous waves and cryptic mists. Shipwrecks, unsurprisingly, are numerous. Serious granite cliffs hold their own against the big weather systems pounding in from the Atlantic Ocean, beautiful inlets and coves beaten by terrific storms and crashing waves. Just north of Land's End, at Cape Cornwall, the Atlantic currents split, south through the English Channel or north into the Bristol Channel and Irish Sea. Where you get seas meeting, you often see wildlife. Up on the cliffs above Lizard Point, a viewing platform nudges visitors to look out for dolphins, whales, turtles and basking sharks in the swirling waters below. At Kynance Cove, grey seals live amid a splendour of shiny dark-green and red serpentine polished by the sea. All this beauty would – as with Durdle Door – be wasted on me; those rocks represented nothing more than a glittering menace. *Isean* and I would not be within three miles of them. I hoped to see wildlife – I always hope to see wildlife – but the sea conditions and potential hazards would be claiming most of my attention. I was up before dawn for the Lizard, my first serious passage alone. I'd studied the tide tables for slack water. I slipped *Isean*'s lines in the lovely quiet of the Helford river and shoved the gear in reverse. The engine quit with a loud bang, reverberating in the still morning air. A try at restarting as we drifted in a busy anchorage. Nothing. I threw the anchor out and paused for thought. It was 6 a.m., a little too early to call even the friendliest of my engineering friends. I checked underneath – there was a rope caught, wrapped tightly and disabling the prop. I slipped into the water, cut it free and started up the trusty Yanmar.

We were off again, sails full, and around Lizard Point. *Isean* flew up and over heavy waves, landing with almighty thuds and groaning from bow to stern with the effort. I turned on the engine and accelerated, but even through the motion and the noise, something felt wrong, the motor whirring but no thrust of power. Then it gave out. Bad timing. My heart sank. I resigned myself to a massive slog: fifteen miles and making barely three knots under sail. The wind shifted ahead, a bit of north now in its west, right in our face as we approached Mount's Bay. Exhausted and in a foul temper, I tacked between Penzance and St Michael's Mount, inching forward. I radioed Newlyn harbour, the only 24-hour shelter in the area, to request a tow at the entrance – no help available. In trepidation, I tried Penzance. They'd be happy to help, but the harbour's locked gate could only open for a limited time. In desperation, I focused the last of my energy, working the helm hard, sailing high to the wind. We got to the entrance just in time, bobbing around with the main up when the friendly little harbour boat came out and made straight for us.

When the engineers in Penzance had a look at the prop, it was bad news. The shaft was bent. So bent that they considered displaying it on the wall. A slight misalignment had seemingly distorted it over time; the rope was the final straw. Worse, the jolt had knocked the engine off its mounts, which now needed to be replaced. I absorbed this bad news with a heavy heart: my budget wasn't ready for such a knock. The immediate feeling when you find a serious problem on your boat is dismay. The next is relief that it didn't fail somewhere terrible. I would not have chosen to lose my engine going round the Lizard – I shouldn't have made the trip. But at least I'd had the sense to stay well offshore, so I'd had sea space, and there had been wind. And I'd been lucky to end up in a proper working harbour, an affordable and interesting place to be. We were in Penzance for five weeks, and there were storms for most of it. I made friends, walked the stunning 'Tin Coast' near St Just, with its old mine ruins, engine houses clinging to the cliffs, tunnels half a mile out to sea – so strange to imagine men working beneath the seabed, waves roaring in their ears. I wandered Penzance and Mount's Bay, this funny little place full of dreamers and doers. The end-to-enders who'd come from John O'Groats to the other extremity. The eccentrics and drifters, people who had simply got the train to the end of the line and stayed. With my passage in mind, I roamed the wild cliff tops, stared out at the storm-battered Longships lighthouse and scanned the sea from every part of the headland I could reach. I took the *Scillonian III* passenger ferry out to the beautiful sandy Scillies. On the way back I was in the wheelhouse – like a kid – picking the skipper's brains about local conditions for rounding the point. I was over-prepared for a passage that I wouldn't make. After all my planning, I never did turn to starboard, to the north. I left Britain. Passage plans change and so did ours. We turned south. Left at Land's End.

The idea of this flight had taken hold during those weeks of waiting. It was impulsive but also weirdly practical. The pause had taken us from July to the end of August, and autumn loomed large. The thought of turning right, and north into winter, no longer held appeal. I met Jim, an experienced sailor, who pointed out the obvious fact that sailing south would be easier than sailing into the Irish Sea. 'It just gets warmer all the way,' he'd said encouragingly. Another lightbulb moment. I called Gary – he knew me, my ability, my little boat – wondering if he'd think it mad. 'Ah, you're in a nice position for a reach all the way down to Spain from there,' was his response. Well, that sounded nice. I stared out to sea. Could I actually do this? Surely I couldn't just sail to Spain? I splashed out on a fixed VHF radio and got a licence to operate it. I bought a life raft. Before I knew it, my preparations were becoming serious. I stared at charts for the Bay of Biscay and I knew I had to do it. I phoned my dad with the news. His voice betrayed disappointment and worry. When you're caught up in your own adventure, it's easy to forget how hard it is for the people you leave behind. He'd been looking forward to me sailing to Scotland. 'What now? Where now?' I was inexperienced. He worried about me being at sea, much less sailing off to Spain. It must be difficult being a parent, watching your children trip their way through life, witnessing all the mistakes, all the learning. How can you ever see them as competent adults? I tried to reassure him that I was more cautious in sailing than in other aspects of my life. I felt some guilt about causing him worry. But I knew that my dad understood. Above all, for me and for my brother David, he wanted only happiness. He could hear in my voice that, with *Isean*, I was finding it.

And I wasn't without worry myself; it was a giant leap. Until five years earlier, I'd barely travelled overseas. I had reached forty, newly single, with six weeks off work and set out on that well-trodden backpacker route to Thailand, Vietnam and Cambodia. A big adventure that exceeded all my expectations, but the thing is, I was really scared before I went. I was scared that I mightn't be safe. That I only spoke English. That I'd be lonely. That I would struggle navigating public transport. Here I was now, about to navigate – really navigate – my way to France and maybe Spain on my own tiny boat. Old fears resurfaced, both emotional and practical. I'd once been daunted by people talking of 'big Brittany seas'. It's natural to fear the unknown and I had been thoroughly put off crossing the Channel some years earlier by their descriptions of monstrous far-off waves. But big Atlantic swells roll into Penzance too – and I'd dealt with those. I thought about my friend Jeff's words on journalism all those years before. 'It's no black art,' he'd said. Sometimes people imply that things they've achieved are mysterious and difficult in order to feel more accomplished themselves. This is rife in sailing. People love to measure journeys in intrepidness – 'If you can sail there,' they say, 'you can sail anywhere!' Warnings should be taken seriously; as I'd learned the hard way, certain places can be especially treacherous. But the truth is there are difficult stretches everywhere, and sometimes the most notorious are benign. It's always – always – about the conditions, the sea state, the weather. What you choose to go out in. The most important thing is to know when not to go. I'd learned that. So it wasn't the sailing, the sea or the weather that most scared me about the crossing. It wasn't even the busy shipping lanes. My biggest fear was that of arriving in an unknown and far-off place. Of being really alone. I was leaving the UK, where I had support, for somewhere I couldn't make myself understood if I needed help. And I would need help because there was so much I didn't know. But I had gained confidence in sailing *Isean*. I'd coped when things went wrong, and what I lacked in technical ability, I made up for in another valuable asset – an uncanny knack of finding good people to help me. I would trust in that. The whole venture was a leap of faith, a foolhardy vote of confidence in myself, in life working out.

What really made leaving okay was *Isean*. I trusted her to keep me safe at sea and to keep me anchored emotionally. I wasn't alone, I was with her. I'd have my home and my comfort with me. Sailors have a special relationship with their boats. It's not only the freedom they represent, the romance of naming them, the undeniable beauty of their lines and curves. It's not just that these few planks of wood keep you from the deadly embrace of an implacable sea. It's more. Our boats take us to the most unimaginable places, but they're not merely a mode of transport. It's not a car, driving a straight line. The boat and the sailor work together, each with their strengths and weaknesses to overcome, through tides and waves, weather and hazards. You know the boat intimately, you care for her every need, having learned the hard way why you must. In return, she does nothing less than keep you safe from harm. Between the two of you, you get there. And yet, it's more still. Once the journey is completed, your boat holds you, safe and comfortable. Perfectly at home in a remote wilderness. How could you not love her? The more time I spent with *Isean*, the more highs and lows we'd endured, the stronger was our bond. She was my companion in adventure, my sanctuary in a storm. I wasn't leaving home at all. My idea of home had changed. It was no longer a location. Life was no longer filled with habits of place; neighbours and friends, the cinema, the local Vietnamese, the weekly shop. I was more interested in browsing shackles and mooring lines in hardware stores than shopping for clothes or homeware. The old routines and distractions had been replaced by the sea's rhythms, the natural world, what we needed to stay safe. *Isean* was home. Wherever she was, was home. Home was my ritual. My journey was home. Every night, the thrill of the new, and my comforts around me. A cup of tea in the morning, the radio on. The water gently lapping and a beautiful view. My tiny shelf of books, a favourite rose-embroidered throw from Paris. A nice dinner. A call to family and friends. My little boat, sitting pretty in pink under sun-stained clouds. It was simple. I had it all; I needed nothing more.

Finally, on the last Saturday in August, as summer rushed to its end, we left Penzance. Ahead, a 24-hour passage to foreign shores; behind, everything I knew. Sailing into the night on a flat-calm sea that reflected my mood. I felt strangely serene, although a little apprehensive with the weight of responsibility. I was taking along an inexperienced crew member I barely knew. She wasn't a sailor, and we were not well matched in the end, but she kept a good watch and allowed me some rest. All experiences are valuable. I learned that I'd rather sail alone than advertise for crew. As we left, just shy of twilight, I looked back. The sun was setting the town ablaze: brilliant golden rays, like autumn come early, the end of a chapter. Crowds of shadowy figures were silhouetted against the harbour wall, hooks and muskets in the air. Tens of thousands of pirates eccentrically marauding the streets of Penzance, an attempt at a world record and a fitting spectacle to mark my last sight of Britain. Strange to go so suddenly, in the end, not even a return to London to collect belongings. I hadn't needed anything for months, I figured; what could I need now? Besides, I didn't know that I'd stay at sea as long as I did. I just knew I had to go.

We headed out and I set the course. 'I'm doing it,' I thought, surprised at myself. It had always seemed a fantastical notion far beyond reach – *one day I'll sail to France*. I was doing it now. Not dreaming. Not waiting for the day I would be ready to do it. It was this day. Out of sight of land and me in charge. Night came carefully, and carefully it went. Cygnus, starry wings flying into the Milky Way. The diamond points of the dolphin, shimmering faintly. Then fading. Dawn light rising; the sky endless in cotton-blue; the sea metallic, Roman silver. I checked my position. On course. I checked myself. On course. With morning, the shipping lanes. Two lanes to cross, some of the world's busiest. Like a stroll across the M25. I'd be glad of the light. Sure enough, on approach, three massive tankers in short succession, each mighty bow wave frothing white with power and speed. I tacked out of their way and quietly thanked the earlier version of me who opted to spend one summer sailing amongst Portsmouth's parade of ships. On a cloudy sea under a watery sunlight, we reached La Manche. French waters. Bye bye, Blighty! I raised the French tricolour. Unflaggy as I am, I still smiled at the symbolism of hoisting a new flag. I was on my way to the Continent. Like the migrating swifts, this bird had flown.

'Isean' she calls me. Little bird. Chick, in the Gaelic, she says. I am a boat, but we too can glide and swoop. A bird, it suits me. But I'm no chick: I've had fifty years. Ages with her. Been around the world. Seen it all. She's the fledgling here. New to the sea. Learning to fly. The mistakes she's made! Wheesht! We'd be home to crabs if it wasn't for me. They all make mistakes, though. It's how they learn. Each mistake once. That's the rule. I've had plenty of beginners and plenty who call themselves experienced, and, believe me, they can be worse.

I've saved her umpteen times. Mind you, she rescued me once. Like a second wind, she lifted me. I thought my sailing days were over. Still in my prime and left high and dry! On the west coast of Scotland; rain, cold and thin. Dreich. Drip drip drip; no salt, no life. Not like the ocean. There I was, so close to the sea, the smell of it hurt. Forgotten. Humans are terrific but people are terrible. I was left behind. Paint flaking, sails stolen. Empty inside. She found me in that state. She was smitten and just like that, my future was bright. And so is hers. We flew south for winter, she and I. So sudden she forgot her winter coat. She thinks she chose this take-off, but I was always pointing that way, ready to unfurl my wings.

To the west, I took her, where the land runs out. And there I waited. I pointed my bow south while she thought north. I would not turn north into winter. The gods saw my plan and they liked it. Thunderstorms cut short summer and held us near autumn. We perched at the very edge of the land that is Britain. Watched the birds set south across the sea. She found the courage to join them. To leave her homeland. It was easier than she imagined. Natural, one night, to follow the kindly sea south with me. A path, lit gold by burning sunset, the shy silver of a waxing crescent moon. Easy in the end, to shake off the safety, the language and customs she knew. So we went. I got my way and it became her way.

6.

The sun was shining bright in the port of l'Aber-Wrac'h and I was revelling in the pleasure of having travelled to another country under my own steam. I hadn't gone to an airport. I hadn't had to show my passport or book a train or exchange money for this journey. I'd just untied *Isean*'s ropes and set off into the sunset – and here we were, surrounded by Plouguerneau oysters and abalones. What a strangely singular freedom. I sat on *Isean*'s bow and was utterly delighted with myself. We had sailed 100 miles, swapping one Land's End for another – Finistère, the north-western corner of Brittany – and were thus resting at the crossroads between the Channel and the Atlantic. A small, balding, agitated man arrived as I chatted happily on the phone, urgently making eye contact as he paced the pontoon for the duration of my call. Evidently losing patience at the wait, he rubbed together his thumb and forefinger at me – the universal sign for money. I cut short the call, thinking he must be the harbour master. But no. He was just impatient to talk – this call, he was signalling, is costing me money, when I could be speaking to him. This was Laga. 'There is only one,' he assured me, several times. Having got my attention, he proceeded to spend forty minutes telling me where I was obliged to sail – the best spots in Brittany – and where to avoid. During this time, his steady artillery fire of questions had found several holes in my outfit. He was aghast that I didn't know about *godiller* – French for sculling – that I hadn't heard of Éric Tabarly, Brittany's sailing great. And he was highly unimpressed when he caught sight of my small bag of cheap tools. Worried I was about to be banished back across the Channel, I offered up my own French sailing hero, the soulful writer Bernard Moitessier. A smile of approval; partially redeemed. Laga was a lighthouse keeper – he had just retired and clearly had time on his hands.

All the navigational markers I'd see in Finistère would have been checked by him. A good thing, for, as I learned, he is rather exacting. The night before, I'd been guided in by his Île Wrac'h lighthouse, standing tall and watching over the estuary – and how relieved I'd been to reach it. I'd been staring for a good couple of hours at its more famous neighbour, Île Vierge, just a mile offshore and unmissable – at over eighty metres, the tallest lighthouse in Europe. It felt like the longest mile I'd ever sailed, racing the setting sun, with strong tides and an offshore wind beating us back after a 24-hour passage. It had been a calm trip, mostly motoring without wind over a flat silvery Channel. Then there was wind – from the land, like a hairdryer, right in the face, impeding our progress so that I wasn't sure our momentum was actually still forward. I went from hoping to get in before dark – okay, the sun has just set – to hoping to get in at all. How much longer, I resentfully wondered, could we fight these conditions? Was there enough fuel? And why, in the name of God, was I out here in the wind and the darkness on a sea that hated me? Which was fine, because the feeling was mutual. By the time we limped up that rock-encumbered estuary, I was too exhausted even to appreciate landing on foreign shores. But that was last night! I'd had some sleep since then and awakened in the entirely novel position of being on my own little boat in France. Sailing was wonderful again. I loved it. Things were all now thoroughly brilliant.

By the harbour, the paternalistic Laga was still complaining about my set-up. 'Your father has let you go to sea with a child's toolbox?' He was right in at least one respect. I didn't have enough tools – and very little equipment in general. Beyond the essential safety gear I'd invested in, it was very basic. I hadn't wanted to fall into the trap so many do: dreaming, working, buying every last bit of gear for every eventuality, preparing for the perfect trip they never make. All over the world, in marinas and harbours, boatyards and backyards, lie fully equipped boats that never go to sea. I wanted to sail. I could add gear along the way. I had no electronic chart plotter. I used chart apps on my phone but I preferred proper charts. If you take care not to get them wet or rip them, they can't go wrong. They don't run out of battery. More than that, though, I actually loved them. This had been a surprising transformation for someone who once detested maps as much as maths, but once I'd learned how to plot, I became besotted. I'd sit with a coffee and all my little tools, like being back in school, the dividers and protractor, the correct pencils – 2B – soft and kind to the chart, and always kept sharp. Thinking about gravitational pull on the water. Those bulging tides, set and drift – direction and speed. Use the compass rose, find the variation between true and magnetic north. All these little rules for the world's big forces – it was so romantic. And so satisfying, to arrive at a definitive direction to steer, to find yourself in exactly that place in real life on shifting seas. I felt like a sorceress on an enchanted boat. Like Circe with magic, magnets and fluid. I became reasonably good at it too, steadily charting lines as we pitched and rolled, wielding my hand-held compass for a three-point fix under way. But after buying and borrowing charts for a good part of the UK, I'd turned south – I couldn't afford more. To my eternal regret, I'd have to rely on the chart apps – I would become one of those skippers glued to their phone. I should get a sextant, learn celestial navigation, pleasingly mystical and extremely practical at once. But I'm worried it might make my head explode.

What else did I lack? An adequate power supply. I had two batteries – the sacred engine starter and a small leisure one. In

Cornwall I'd bought two tiny solar panels – totalling a minuscule forty watts and performing at half that. It offered just enough power to charge my phone, the anchor light and a wireless speaker. In that order. My phone was crucial for navigation, weather and communication. If there was no sun, then I'd do without music and podcasts. I had to conserve energy for safety at sea – the best motivation. I turned into everyone's dad – 'Is that light off?' – obsessive about power waste, a discipline that will never leave me. I'm happy about that. A friend visiting in Falmouth was incredulous. 'But you have . . . nothing,' he'd said. True, there was not much comfort on board. There was no fridge. No heating. I had a radar reflector but no Automatic Identity System to transmit my position (I'd regret this when fog descended). My depth gauge was a bit iffy but my compass was good – unsure of depth but certain of direction. 'Twas ever thus. I was happy with fewer things to break. I'd spent long enough on what I did have, my head in the oily bilges changing the electric pump, or my head in the 'heads', becoming familiar with the inner workings of my sea toilet. The living space was about that of a classic VW campervan. It was camping, really. What I did have was a two-burner hob and grill, a kitchen sink and a leaky water tank, lockers for food, pots and pans. My fridge was a bag thrown into the sea on a rope. My clothes were bundled into the forepeak, which also housed a toilet, sink and a locker where toiletries mingled with first-aid supplies. I had a narrow berth to sleep on. If I wanted to read at night, I had my miner's headlamp, but usually I fell asleep in a fit of happy exhaustion after sailing, book discarded by my side. I had everything I needed, the kind of simplicity that allows real freedom. And I had emotional support in contact with friends. You're a worry when you're sailing alone, for those you leave behind. So many stories of solo sailors lost overboard – a careless step in rough conditions and no one to haul you back on board. It's usual, on long passages, to check in with someone who knows your route, your departures and estimated arrivals. When I left Britain I started a group chat with my nearest and dearest – Cat, Phil and Saoirse. More than a safety check, it became a record of highs and lows, shared joys and sorrows, my many complaints and tantrums. They cheered me up and they cheered me on as I made my way south.

Smillie's people

SAOIRSE: Hey buddy! How you doing? Still sailing?

SUSE: Ten miles to go and wind in my face OF COURSE. Soooo tired.

SAOIRSE: Hang in there! Let us know when you've arrived.

PHIL: Can you get a cup of tea?

SUSE: NO TEA :(Autohelm quit and I can't get off helm. I peed in a bucket. No tea for 12 hours. SOBBING.

SUSE: Anchor set! Look at my view!!! It's SO GOOD. I have tea and biscuit!!! Yay!

PHIL: Looks nice. Are you protected from swell?

CAT: Wooooo! Gorgeous! I looked it up, LOOK AT THIS BEACH ROUND THE CORNER. That water! Dive in!!!

I used social media too. The tribal nature of online communities and algorithms mean we can end up in echo chambers, something I'm keen to reduce, but when you're travelling alone, like-minded people are exactly what you want. It was so helpful, other sailors sharing forecasts and local tips. I posted a lot, for company and connection, as well as a record and diary, a kind of online ship's log. I often used it too much. When I was scrolling images of dolphins one morning, a bottlenose dolphin surfaced for a second under my bow, then was gone. I have never felt a bigger fool. Ignoring your surroundings to look at pictures is bad; taking photographs of the world around you is better, but even here you have to be careful. I've become a bit addicted to that too. 'Turn the phone off, just enjoy this,' I'd scold myself. But I found my perspective changing with the camera, looking up close, appreciating the wonder of detail in everyday things. Counter-intuitively, using the camera taught me to look more carefully without it, to focus on the beauty that exists in the least likely of places, my mind's eye zooming in to frame wild flowers springing from scrubland, sea-skating insects, thread legs delicately balanced on the surface. It's made me feel safer too, my camera. I've used it as a weapon and a shield. Just looking at some situations through a lens helps to distance them emotionally. I've taken refuge in my camera as a shark headed for me underwater and when a ship headed for me above water, the frame making both feel less real. In dodgy situations with humans, I've often pressed 'record', and although I've never done it, I've often imagined live-streaming as a kind of protection when there's no other. So many times, a camera has made me feel less alone.

In fact, this fear of being alone was unfounded. I rediscovered what all travellers know – there are brilliant people everywhere. They make the places you go. I loved the Bretons right away. They're crazy about sailing and this predisposed me towards them. From the moment I arrived, I was pulled into company, into homes, comfort offered and friendship extended without hesitation. It reminded me of my upbringing. My childhood home was also open-door, my dad always trailing strangers into the kitchen. It came naturally to him. He grew up with his mother Roseanne inviting the rag women and street singers of Kirkintilloch in to sit by the fire and tell their stories. My mum was equally welcoming, always with a ready laugh and a pot of soup 'on the go'. They had an easy warmth that invited you in, my parents; a love big enough to share. In Brittany I found a similar familial fraternity. There was no reserve, no distance. As a woman sailing alone, I was received with kindness and interest in this most seafaring of regions. At times it unnerved me, as with the seasoned sailor in Brest who told me how brave I was to take on the 'nose of Brittany' by myself. You never want to be told that you're brave ahead of a passage. Afterwards? Yeah, bring it on, but not before. Generally, though, the collective response was 'Bravo!'

That was how I met Antoine, in the sea just outside Loctudy. An avid sailor, he raced over in his classic dinghy, offering his hand over *Isean*'s guard rails. 'Scottish!' he exclaimed at my accent as he displayed the salt-crusted cuffs of his Shetland jumper. By the time I'd got into the harbour and tied up, he'd called his wife, busy preparing a dinner party for friends. 'She's invited,' Nicole had said. He swept me up, salty, hungry, tired, took me home and pushed me into the bathroom with clean towels. By the time I came out, showered and warm, I had a pair of slippers and an aperitif waiting by the armchair, home-cured anchovies, spiced langoustines, Antoine's special plum tart. As I looked at his sailing pictures on the wall, I noticed a photograph of a beautiful girl – their grown-up daughter. They lost her, he told me. Simple words for an unspeakable pain. The abyssal hurt of losing a child. I'd seen it take my parents to the depths, a different pain from my own, but I understood its character, its stubborn endurance, the magnitude of it. I was drawn into Antoine and Nicole's extended family that night, sitting around the dinner table with their musician friends, chatting and laughing until the early hours. When I met them at Loctudy market the next day, they'd bought me a pair of blue-and-white-striped wool slippers. Little emblems of kindness that would find a place snuggling up to *Isean*'s mast at the centre of the saloon, making her more homely. They became part of my ritual. I slipped into them every morning, yawning in the darkness of dawn departures, padding around with my coffee. I wore them with shorts when autumn's shy sun left decks clinging with dew till noon. I wore them long after I had to, appreciating more than their warmth. I remember after we lost Stephen and I'd gone back to university, I'd spent months in a woolly hat, falling asleep drunk in it, waking up in it, hungover and broken in bed. My hangover hat. I don't know why I did that. Maybe it was a kind of comfort blanket. I wasn't sad any more but I loved these charming *chaussons* hugging my feet, a reminder that where there was enormous pain, there was huge capacity for love and kindness.

Back in l'Aber-Wrac'h, my new friend Laga had summoned me to his home. His patient wife made me coffee while he showed me all the things he'd made – a list that included a boat, his shed and his house – and the giant telescope he kept trained on the port. I wouldn't stay late, I was up early the next day. We were edging farther into autumn and I had a loose plan to meet Gary in Lorient, from where we'd cross the Bay of Biscay to Spain, but before that I had two major tidal passages to tackle alone – the Chenal du Four and the notorious Raz de Sein. I had checked the following day's forecast for the first – light winds in the morning, building in the afternoon – I'd be up early and off to Brest. A little daunted by what lay ahead, I was receptive when Laga offered to come. 'Are you sure?' his wife exclaimed in surprise. 'Laga, on the boat with you . . . all day?' I looked at her doubtful expression, their daughter Amélie quietly smirking. I realised he hadn't stopped talking since verbally accosting me on arrival. The three of us laughed, as he looked on, half amused, half baffled. 'Maybe not,' I thought again. Off I went, after sunrise, alone and no doubt under his watchful telescopic eye.

Smillie's people

SUSE: Bonjour! I'm on the approach to the Chenal du Four!!!
   Timed it perfectly, tide just turning. XITED!!!
SUSE: Ah. Wait. The engine has just gone. Hmm.

SUSE: I'll have to sail!

PHIL: Through the channel? Isn't it all rocks and reefs?

SUSE: I reckon it'll be fine, the wind is steady.

PHIL: But really strong tides pushing you around. Sounds risky?

SUSE: Nooooooo! The wind's dropped away to nothing! I can't sail.

SUSE: SHIT. MIST. There's no wind and it's misty. FFS.

PHIL: Shit. Radio the coastguard. Tell them you're alone without engine.

PHIL: You need a tow.

PHIL: Suse. Are you okay?

The good news was we didn't seem to be getting sucked into the channel. 'That's a positive,' I told *Isean* as she bobbed by the entrance in the mist. 'Stay like that.' I opened the engine bay and stared hard – more in hope than anything. Air in the system, I thought. I had never bled the engine, but there wasn't time to convince myself I couldn't do it. Against my own odds, I managed and was applauded by the cheering put-put of my little motor. We went into the Chenal and were through in no time. A few hours later, we rounded up to north, into the Rade de Brest and a building wind, thirty-knot gusts overpowering us. Harness on. Up I went, crawling over the coachroof. Blasted by sea spray, umbilically attached to *Isean*, I reduced the mainsail and crawled back to the helm. *Isean* was now perfectly balanced and sailing beautifully. I stared up as we shot past the Pointe des Espagnols. I was on a total high, drunk on adrenaline, a little bit smug. We veered off, seeking shelter. The wind swerved round the headland with us and my elation was fast turning to exhaustion. It had been a long day; forty miles, twelve hours of hard physical graft. I just wanted to stop. I grabbed a mooring buoy but couldn't keep a grip as a strong tide tried to wrench my arm off. It did not go well.

Smillie's people

SUSE: I almost crashed.

SAOIRSE: What? No! Are you okay?

SUSE: I was on the bow and the helm jammed.
I almost slammed a boat.

PHIL: Oh shit! The boat's all right?

SUSE: Isean's fine. I'm so stupid. I should have rigged
lines to the cockpit.

SUSE: I'm a shit sailor.

SAOIRSE: You're not a shit sailor. You're a tired sailor.

SUSE: It was so close. I hate myself.

PHIL: Oh Suse. Isean is fine and you're safe. Make a cuppa.
I'm calling you.

Sometimes, the lessons come hard and fast. I'd been so proud of myself flying up towards Brest. I'd sailed to France two days before. I'd just done the Chenal du Four, alone. I'd fixed my engine, reduced sail under way. Then I almost crashed my beautiful boat through sheer stupidity. And that got me: how easily my dreams could have been shattered, the trip over, the boat lost. I felt utterly disgusted with myself, but too exhausted to dwell on my shortcomings. I had to be up early the next morning and over to Brest to spend the day rushing around after the tiny whirlwind that is Laga. He had driven twenty miles just to help me clean my fuel tank. 'I am on holiday all the time now,' he said, refusing the money I offered as he drove me around getting bits. For such a small man, he can really shift, darting everywhere at breakneck speed in a torrential downpour. I literally ran behind while he shouted at me all day – 'SuZANNE!' – about how bad my spanners were or why my socket set was a child's one. We ran down to the port, where his former colleagues tramped around forlorn navigation markers in for repair and beamed sympathetically at me, Laga's hapless new friend, on some mad journey. That was the last time I saw him, this small lighthouse man, dwarfed by giant yellow cardinal buoys, his eyes flashing amongst the broken lights. *Isean* and I hopped off to the quiet of Camaret to prepare for our passage through the Raz de Sein, which I was taking very seriously indeed. Its lighthouse, La Vieille, must have been intimately known to Laga. In every picture I saw — and there were many, for it's the kind of diabolically photogenic place that turns up often in those epic storm posters you see — it was being battered by waves so infernal that surely there was only one — the one Laga — capable of tending it.

I'd been thinking more like a sailor since arriving in France. Thinking farther ahead. Considering conditions in the coming days, weather and tides, the best chance of a stress-free passage. I was staring at the moon. I did not want that captivating silver disc that shone full above *Isean*'s mast. It brought powerful spring tides. I wanted half of it. Days away. But not too many. And I wanted a day without strong winds. I'd have to time it just right. The tides here were strong and the swell was substantial. I'd read several accounts of sudden fog descending on the turning of the tide as colder water from below meets warm air. This is the calmest period, and exactly when you want to go through. I thought about the fog that came so suddenly, as the tide turned at the Chenal du Four. I watched that full moon wane gibbous and I huffed over contradictory weather forecasts. I'd learned to check forecasts but not to rely on them — they can miss local conditions, and sea state is affected by weather systems many hundreds of miles away. At Camaret I listened to the *Shipping Forecast*, checked my wind and wave apps, and went to sleep as local forecasts transmitted on the VHF radio, listening for '*force du vent*' or '*tempête*'.

I was up early, a little trepidatious, and off before dawn. A cheery fishing boat was coming into port, the sky turning from black to navy blue. The last of the stars twinkled in counsel and companionship – 'Enjoy it, enjoy it, we'll see you tonight.' I was among friends. The sunrise brought light breezes and a flat-calm sea, and I hoped it would last. It did. The Raz was a massive anticlimax, the best kind. Entirely benign. No big waves. No fog. No engine problems. No adventure to regale and no regrets. A passage made memorable precisely for its lack of drama. It marked a big point in my journey, a step forward in my sea education. I had planned it well. Conditions had been so perfect I was sunbathing on deck as *Isean* left that notorious lighthouse in our wake. I will never forget the giddy mix of relief and pride, looking to stern as I lay smiling in the sunshine. The Raz, you say? No big deal. Up to Audierne and the Goyen river. The following day was blustery, all white horses at sea, the harbour walls holding us in a strong embrace. I looked at the webcam over the Raz de Sein. I expect it looked rough. I couldn't tell. It was opaque. Swathed in heavy fog as the deafening sea roared out of sight. I shuddered over my *moules-frites*, gripped the stem of my second massive glass of *vin blanc* and drained it in a fug of happy relief.

Everything about the Atlantic felt *grande* in Brittany. Enormous fish – tuna perhaps – leaping out of a vast sea. The swell was big, memorably so. I passed a large fishing boat one day, and it completely disappeared from view as giant waves rolled hypnotically between us. I laughed, thinking about what we must have looked like in the belly of the trough, just the tip of *Isean*'s mast poking out. The ocean was kind to us, though. They were beautiful waves, and they had come a long way across the Atlantic. Dark and silver-crested, slow and sweeping, big but forgiving. Gentle beasts. We raced a storm to Lorient and waited out bad weather. Here we were, *Isean* and I, in the Bay of Biscay. This huge bay – some 350 miles across – is home to some of the Atlantic Ocean's worst conditions. Parts of the continental shelf extend far inside the bay, creating sudden drops in depth and abnormally high waves in rough weather. We had arrived in mid-September, just at the end of the recommended season for crossing. I negotiated with my insurers to extend cover, reasoning that as the final days of their window to cross were blighted by raging storms, I'd wait for better weather and sail with a professional offshore skipper – Gary was coming. They agreed. We set off for Spain late one September evening on an inky sea, a crescent moon and stars above. Out to the Bay of Biscay.

It feels different, deep water. Safer in many ways – no rocks to hit, few hazards to worry you, lots of space. This vast dark sea. It was home once, wasn't it? We're related to starfish. A few evolutionary wriggles and it's unnerving now, to be out of depth and far from land. We've forgotten what lies beneath. We worship at the foot of the Himalayas, yet know nothing of the ocean's deep canyons, valleys and ridges, its abyssal hills and plains. How breathtaking they too must be. The Mid-Atlantic Ridge, whose peaks include the verdant Azores, is more than double the length of the Andes. Oceanic trenches dig deeper than the earth's mountains reach up. Place Mount Everest in the Mariana Trench, and miles of Pacific would wash above her peak. Crossing the Bay of Biscay is not crossing an ocean – you're days, not weeks from landfall – but it's farther than I had ever been, far enough when you think about it. We headed out from Lorient, over the continental shelf. About a hundred miles south-west, the depth goes from a hundred metres to a thousand and up. In response, the instruments went on strike, *Isean*'s dodgy depth gauge sending its erratic little signal out, looking for the seabed, bouncing back dizzy with vertigo. Sure enough, canyons plunged below. Deeper than I could imagine. I felt like a crumb, floating on the surface, nothing below for miles. Nothing above either: no land, no other boats for three days, no one in sight or radio range. A real wilderness. No sign that humans ever existed, no floating nets or oil rigs; none of Laga's light-houses or cardinal markers out here, nothing made by human hand. And no light pollution. Nothing to distract from winking stars, the wash of the Milky Way. When I was little, with a mess of spiral hair, my dad always sang to me. A song to the moon: 'Ma Curly-Headed Baby'. Still tiny, I learned to recognise the big old record that played it. Paul Robeson, a true polymath, the African American bass baritone, actor, athlete, lawyer, activist – and my dad's hero. I used to pull it out from the stacks of 78s, begging for it to be played. Then I learned how to lift the heavy old vinyl disc and place the gramophone needle. I played it over and over again. I could feel the song as much as hear it. Robeson's deep voice rumbling through the trumpet horn, vibrating with warmth. '*Do you want the moon to play with / or the stars to run away with*.' Out there, staring up at a sky cluttered with stars, I'd found them. Like my dad always promised. '*They'll come if you don't cry.*' I relied upon them, like friends, to keep us on course. Not the bright North Star. I prefer the seven-starred Plough, the hindquarters of Homer's Bear. Keep it just to the left of *Isean*'s mast, check the moon. Is she still at my port quarter aft? Then we're heading in the right direction.

But remember, the moon also rises, the earth is rotating, its poles wandering; everything is moving, nothing is still. The stars were showily shooting overhead, but they couldn't compete, for I was staring down where dolphins were so clearly lit by bioluminescence that I hardly trusted my eyes. I'd seen them come from a distance, streaking through the water. I couldn't have missed them. Flying along beside me were the dark and white curving lines of this wonderful mammal, lit pale green by tiny creatures. I was in a trance, leaning over the side, left hand on the tiller, my right arm shoulder-deep in that magical ocean, reaching down. I felt a hypnotic pull into the water, so lost in the moment that the luffing of the sails made me jump. I looked skywards for the Plough. We had a long way to go. I couldn't afford to go off course already. I tried to steer, keep my bearings. Suddenly, close beside me, a dolphin broke the surface, forcefully expelling air as if trying to get my attention, to draw me back down there. Maybe it thought I was a selkie. I wished I was. I would have flown along beside it forever. Off we went like this, three hundred miles ahead, *Isean* merrily lilting under a smiling crescent moon, dolphins glistening alongside, all of us running away with the stars.

7

A battered little fleet of boats lined up in Spain's Marina Coruña, their flags too wet to flap – British ensigns, French tricolours, the Nordic cross. Clearly they'd just crossed the Bay of Biscay too. Bedding and cushions airing on decks, waterproofs hanging heavily on booms, soggy clothes strewn and gear piled along the pontoon; everything everywhere, everything waterlogged. Sleeping bodies slumped, and worn-out figures like me trekking off into the old city; no sightseeing for us, just maintenance and repairs to work through. One boat looked worse than the rest, flying a Welsh flag, the foresail hanging in torn ribbons. It had staggered in a few hours after us, caught out by the violent gales that we narrowly escaped. Our journey had been enough of a slog, blighted by small problems and big winds in the final hours. The autohelm quit. As did the bilge pump, and the engine. And my phone, its life cut short in oily bilge water. I had bled the Yanmar – an expert now – as we battered through waves, my hands scratched and bruised, diesel spilling into the open cuts. I was exhausted, stalking Gary obsessively as he slept, praying for the movement that signalled my turn to rest. I'm not sure I'd make a great offshore sailor. After just three days of nothing but sea, I was delighted to be awakened at dawn by conversation on the radio – 'cuanto costa' – Spanish trawlers outside my window and the Galician coast in the near distance. Hola España! We might be in by lunchtime: showers – duchas! – tapas, cerveza in the sunshine. Then the wind started to build, right on our nose, like clockwork. A lunchtime ETA shifted to dinnertime as we slogged away. I was glad of Gary's company as well as his skill, pointing expertly into wind. Soon, rain was hammering as relentlessly as the bloody south-westerly, a nice reminder of my need for sailing gear that is actually waterproof. It was near midnight when we got to La Coruña, exhausted, cold and hungry. *Nada.* No restaurants open. The showers were shut. Everything was shut. The boat was upside down, there wasn't much food left and the gas had run out. I was far too tired and dejected to cook anyway. Rather than prepare meals in advance, I'd been cooking all the way across the bay on an extreme – and very silly – culinary rodeo. Wielding a sharp knife to shave garlic, slice chilli, zest lemon – can't forget the lemon zest – as the boat pitched and heeled. I'd felt guilty about the misery of our arrival, but things always look brighter with sleep.

We woke to sunshine, headed for *tapas* and – finally – Gary got a cold bottle of pale Estrella Galicia, before I saw him off in a cab and wandered back to *Isean*. Soon I heard my name yelled enthusiastically across the marina. Cat, a grin as wide as the bay itself, out to join me on her first proper sail. 'You sailed to Spain, Smillie!' Yes! I did! I had been gratified that in the crossing with Gary there were no decisions I hadn't made myself, no action I wouldn't have taken alone. I had learned a lot. A couple of days putting *Isean* back together and we were off. I was in even more of a rush. We were now well into the second half of September. Winter was coming, and with it, the wild Atlantic storms that batter this exposed coast. I wanted to get south to shelter ahead of them. My ultimate plan was less formulated: I'd decided to get to the bottom of Portugal and swing round to the Algarve, where I'd hopefully find a free anchorage. I had expected help from the Nortada – the Portuguese trade wind – blowing us nicely all the way down, but I'd seemingly just missed it. The wind, when it blew, was ahead of us, so progress would remain stubbornly slow. Which was unfortunate, given we were on the Costa da Morte. White crosses on the jagged cliffs above marked the resting places of numerous shipwrecks; skeletons lurked in the depths.

And there was a bigger problem than the southerly wind. I'd heard this was a foggy place. I'd heard right. Five hours of thick fog accompanied us all the way around Finisterre – like Brittany's Finistère, from the Latin – *finis*, 'end', and *terrae*, 'land'. This place, though, was once more than the end of land. Thought to be the most westerly point of mainland Europe (actually Portugal's Cabo da Roca), Galicia's Finisterre was considered the end of the known world by the Romans. It's a desolate and beautiful cape, a place of myth and legend, a destination for pilgrims. Up there at the cliff edges, rocks are blackened with scorch marks from clothes burnt in a ritual of rebirth; a sculpted bronze boot overlooks the Atlantic. Thousands of people over thousands of years have come to these cliffs to stare out at the gateway to the afterlife. Far below, we were making our way on a little boat through thick fog, edging blindly into another realm. What started as atmospheric turned eerie, then miserable. We hugged the coast, hoping to avoid big ships in deeper water. Over the entire passage, the VHF radio transmitted mournful calls on channel 16 for a boat reported missing; it had disappeared in rough weather here the night before. On the hour, every hour, the coastguard's sombre voice penetrated the fog, a distant cry from another world. With each call, our hopes for their crew diminished. Cat's face registered the same solemnity I felt. She returned my sad smile, both of us considering the futility of looking out for anything in this void. 'Maybe they're tucked up safely,' I offered. 'They might not know they're missing. Someone will spot their boat in a harbour and soon the calls will stop.' But on it went, this disembodied voice, a helpless plea for contact, swirling through the mist. We were quiet, moving slowly, Cat on helm while I shivered on the bow. Run-down from all my rushing and in the beginnings of a fever, I stared intently into nothingness, foghorn in hand. Visibility was reduced to just a few boat-lengths. At one point, the ghostly spectre of a fishing boat, a mini-*Mary Celeste*, suddenly loomed out of nowhere, lurking silently in the gloom like a mirage but dangerously real. Cat – evidently a natural – veered quickly to avoid it. At another point, the fog momentarily cleared over a crescent of beach that looked so close I panicked, thinking we were about to run aground. This time it was an illusion – the charts showed the bay was half a mile off. Fog and mist play havoc with perspective, particularly when you're already spooked and in the beginnings of a fever. I was grateful not to be alone. I was especially glad to have Cat, undaunted by anything life throws at her. Most people would have hated this sail through enveloping mist. Not her. She's followed the salt traders of the Himalayas, spent weeks trekking with caravans through high passes in heavy snowfall, camera fingers freezing, eyelashes stuck together. Like Shackleton, she'd give you her ration of biscuits if you were failing in the freezing ice. A few hours in coastal fog was nothing. 'I'm so glad I'm here,' she shuddered in the cold. 'It's beautiful, but it would be WEIRD for you, in here alone.' Gradually – thankfully – the density dropped, the fog thinning and dissipating until we saw it from the other side, a thick white halo. 'Did you notice?' Cat murmured. 'The calls have stopped.' The radio had fallen silent, as if it had been a bad dream, a loop playing over and over in the otherworld. We told ourselves the boat had been found safe and well, and looked back at the fog-bow blanketing Finisterre. It was mesmerising, this celestial light, but we left it gladly for the warm embrace of a more earthly atmosphere.

By the time we reached the mountainous Cíes Islands, it was a shifting mist. Shafts of sunlight picked out lush-green forests and oyster-white beaches, fleeting glimpses of paradise in the Galicia national park. 'Look how beautiful it probably is!'

shouted Cat, ever the optimist. She changed into a bikini for the few seconds that the sun penetrated. I threw her a blanket. We anchored. I collapsed in the cockpit, aching and barely moving for hours. My energy was all but gone. Cat cooked, noting I'd lost weight. She outlined the importance of eating well to fuel the physical expedition that she reminded me I was on. It wasn't just sitting on a boat; it was hard work. She was right. I knew this as a skipper – the importance of preparing food before conditions deteriorate and you're caught up in physical effort you don't have the energy for. It was a subject she was familiar with and it was a theme she'd return to when I messaged, exhausted under way and fighting the elements. 'You have to eat before you set out,' she'd say. 'Yes, even if you're not hungry.' We rowed to Illa do Faro, deserted in late September, for gentle walks among pristine pine forests. Thanks to the fog and my fever, it was an unusually quiet time for us. Generally Cat turns up in a rush of energy, the pair of us loud with laughter for days, conversations spilling late into nights. Her visits were as welcome as a warm wind pushing from behind. I was always happy to be joined by friends on the way, but some were easier than others. It can be difficult to accommodate people. It isn't just sharing the tiny space; it's the logistics. Weeks of guessing where I might be as I inch my way around coastlines, impeded by weather and life. Which airport, where to pick them up and drop them off. People need certainty ahead of a flight. Except Cat. Cat doesn't need anything. 'Okay, you'll be near Portugal by then,' she'd smile down the phone. 'I'll find you!' She isn't a sailor, but understands how hard the sea can be. She's seen me take on risky conditions and hurt myself or *Isean* rushing to drop people at a location that was convenient for them. Sailing when you shouldn't. I was learning to do what was right for the boat first. Cat's visits, she determined, should always help me on my way. I'd be anchored off a tiny town on the edge of nowhere, no trains, no buses, just a plan, made fast and loose, for her to join me – and I'd hear her before I saw her, emerging from the Iberian hills like a nimble ibex: 'Woooo, my Smillie!' A small figure waving from land, a bag on her back and a camera. She got me through this nasty corner of wind and fog, gave me a morale boost, and then off she went, back into the old quarter of Vigo, the last stop in Atlantic Spain. *Isean* and I tripped across the border, butterflies fluttering, dolphins racing, and a little bird, its feathered chest heaving delicately as it landed, hitching a ride to Portugal.

Here, the Iberian peninsula stretches south through miles and miles of empty coastline, surf-lashed sea cliffs and sweeping white sands. Utterly idyllic, but less than fun for a small boat looking for shelter. There are enough quays and marinas for day-sailing, but you have to plan carefully. I'd read that strong currents rushing out of rivers and meeting a big Atlantic swell can cause standing waves. I'd heard of fatalities as skippers tried to enter harbours in the wrong conditions. Which is why sensible people observe an important rule on the way down this coast – if in doubt, stay out. The decision can be made for you – many harbours close during bad storms. It sounds horribly cruel to be turned away from shelter in a storm, but conditions can make it too dangerous to attempt entry. If you don't get in ahead of deteriorating weather, you're stuck out there at the mercy of the raging Atlantic. Of all the mistakes I had made along my way – and there were many – being left out at sea in a massive Atlantic storm was the one error I absolutely wouldn't be making. I didn't know enough about weather and sea state – I still don't – but I knew to pay close attention, to consult several sources. And to leave room for error. I would estimate the journey time, then set off earlier, always trying to arrive at my destinations on high water and with light.

I reached Aveiro on a full moon and strong spring tides. It's a colourful place, the Little Venice of Portugal, they say – brightly painted *barcos moliceiros* ferry tourists around its maze of canals, all ornate bridges and houses in primary stripes of yellow, blue, green, red. Not that I could see it. Like clockwork: fog. It's a busy commercial port. Rather than risk meeting a hulking great ship in the haze, I decided to wait for visibility to improve before attempting entry. I drifted around in a bit of a daze, a foggy dreamlike state, my thinking slowed, distance and time distorted. Dozens of fishermen dotted the entrance on tiny boats. They all appeared to be moving backwards in slow motion, fishing off the stern of their boats, like a misty merry-go-round or the stall at a fête where you hook toy fish. The blanketing silence made it still more unreal. On the harbour wall, a candy-striped lighthouse was adding a nice funfair effect to proceedings. But hang on, it was moving. Its red and white stripes swirling and shifting in the mist. A floating lighthouse? Was it real? Wait. No, it was not moving. I was moving, had moved; quite fast, in fact. We were being sucked in, *Isean* and I. In response to my daydreaming, strong currents had made the decision for me. We'd now be entering the port during the fog, not after it. It was too surreal to get nervous, and my brain wasn't working fast enough to entertain fear. I wasn't running this show. *Isean* had taken over. Magically, we edged past ghostly figures of men fishing, half-imagined shadows of boats drifting through the mists of time. Perhaps that's why they paint Aveiro in bright stripes of colour – in the hopes of being seen through the bloody fog. A few days in its clammy grip and on I pressed, cold and tired. At Figueira da Foz, I had a short but welcome reprieve. A clear evening, on my way up the Mondego river, appreciating the novelty of being able to see, I turned to ascertain what was making the unholy racket behind me. Gulls, in biblical numbers, like a sky filled with locusts, screaming around a fishing boat, the sun a ball of golden fire sinking into the sea behind. An extraordinary spectacle at any time, but my scene-starved eyes feasted on this sight. I stared, so awestruck I didn't even mind bouncing in the trawler's considerable wake as it tore past. I did well to appreciate that warm golden sunset, that sky full of birds. The skies would soon fill with wind, fire and smoke. Ophelia was coming. The first category-three-strength hurricane ever recorded on this side of the Atlantic was barrelling its way east.

Storm forecasts focus your mind. Especially when you can't cover distance at speed. Difficult decisions need to be made early and fast. If you can't escape its orbit, or its direction is uncertain, the remaining choice is where to ride it out. Do you head for a crowded harbour or opt to anchor in a spot with sea space? Whatever you decide, it feels like a bad choice in the final hours. In the case of a hurricane, it's mainly praying it won't hit, hoping the worst will veer off or blow itself out at sea. I usually love a harbour in a storm, but in something of this strength, all bets are off – you might just be smashed against other boats, the pontoons, sea-defence walls. Where it hasn't been cleared or degraded, nature offers better defences – the creeks and inlets, hurricane holes, protected by reefs and mangroves. Backwaters and rivers winding into the countryside, cushioned with soft yielding mud. The womb-like security of a dandy hole. Even if I could have reached somewhere suitable, I lacked experience, and I doubt I'd have the courage to sit things out by myself in a hurricane. I'd be feeling like the loneliest boat in the world, panicking about my holding, my anchor, my chain. Wishing I was in a harbour. While your boat might be damaged in port, your life will likely be safe. At the first sniff of trouble, I ran straight for harbour walls and the company of my fellow human beings, for what I knew. In a madly counter-intuitive move, I headed for Nazaré, a big surf mecca roughly halfway down Portugal's coast, and home to some of the most powerful waves on the planet. Dense walls of water tower over a hundred feet as they curl terrifyingly towards Praia do Norte. When you look at the charts for this area, something stands out. A long band of shade, like a witch's finger – the Nazaré Canyon, a submarine crack that reaches three miles deep – pointing from 140 miles out, straight to the helpless little town. Galactic Atlantic swells roll in here, all that terrible energy speeding just a few metres from the beach. But Nazaré, strangely enough for a place with a vertiginous underwater canyon and unspeakable waves, has that rare thing on this coast – a safe harbour with all-weather access. Certainly there's enough water for entry at all states of tide.

There is a real camaraderie among sailors when serious weather is coming. You can feel everyone weighing up their situation – boat, equipment, budget, personal approach to risk – then you see it, in progress that's purposeful, the sails reefed, the engines on. People take time to smile and wave or grimace and shrug, making signs that all mean the same thing: 'Good luck, what can we do, hope we're okay.' I called ahead – there was still room in the marina. We got in and tied up, watched the skies darken, as more boats arrived, each in a little puff of relief. I went about my storm preparation, pulled *Isean* well back from the pontoon in the hope she wouldn't smack into it. Double moored, front lines, aft and spring lines to take the strain. Another line off from midships. All the fenders out to protect the hull. I fretted about my half hitches and bowline knots, those lines that were slightly frayed, cleats that were a bit weak. I tied down everything I didn't want to lose. Then I turned to worrying about things beyond my control – the unoccupied boats that might crash into me, the pontoon and how well it was fixed to its concrete bases. It's horrible waiting for a big storm: the calm before, the electricity in the air, the tension. Confronting the reality of how small and fragile we are in the face of something like that. It drives home the loss of those natural habitats too, when you long for protection that is no longer there. It's no longer academic, but a source of deep personal regret. We only really pay attention when things affect us directly.

We weathered the winds overnight, my anxiety rising and waning along with Ophelia. After gaining strength just south of the Azores, 700 miles away, the hurricane weakened to our west and was an ex-hurricane by the time it hit. It was wild enough, though. The following morning, the skies above Nazaré's red-roofed houses filled with thick black smoke that blotted out the sun. Extreme heat and recent droughts had left fields parched and eucalyptus trees as dry as tinder. Wildfires had started and the flames, fanned by Ophelia's high winds, were spreading fast. Over the next few days, local fire crews battled searing heat to quell ferocious flames. Some twenty-seven people lost their lives. Homes were destroyed, fertile land ruined. Those forests, once a valuable carbon sink, were now releasing planet-warming gases into the air. It was strange to sail away from the earth on fire. When I awoke the next morning, my phone was full of pictures from friends in London. People in the UK had woken to abnormal orange skies, like a scene from *Blade Runner*. Overnight that smoke, whipped together with Saharan sand, had been blown north by Ophelia. In just a few hours the pollution had flown from where *Isean* and I sailed, following our journey back home. A visual reminder of how closely our fates are linked, how much smaller the planet is than we imagine, how pointless our boundaries. Winds and currents carry their cargo without need for customs, pay no heed to borders. In my mind, borders were already insignificant at sea anyway, imaginary human lines on a chart. Unlike real barriers that exist in nature — a reef, a tidal race, a sandbank — I crossed these meaningless places without notice. At sea, I was beginning to feel more like part of the natural world, to understand my precarious place within it. I was learning to value its rules over the laws and systems we've created.

We grow up in built environments that seem so permanent, we think that's the world. As a kid, I didn't notice nature pushing through; now I see nothing but. The signs are always there, in flowers growing through cracks in walls, rivers breaking defences, tarmacked roads bulging and boiling with tree roots. The longer I spent at sea, the madder seemed our attempts at control, how we set ourselves above and apart from nature. Even our language is upside down. I sailed along the coast, looking back to toxic skies over the land, listening to the radio and growing incensed as politicians talked about the storm, the future, about being in a battle with nature. I felt like phoning them up in a salty rant to tell them they were wrong, that we are a part of nature, that we must work with it. As if I was living one of those terrible inspirational quotes. 'I'm beating into gale-force winds,' I'd shout manically, wind whistling, waves crashing, 'but I can change course, trim my sails, turn round, and the wind and waves will drive me from behind and now everything's quiet. Do you hear? Do you see?' That night on anchor I read UK newspapers jokingly referring to the apocalypse, running reassuring explanations about smoke and sand and wind. For people staring at the strange phenomena, those disaster-film skies, explanations were helpful, but the facts were hardly encouraging. With the projected increase of extreme weather events, a tropical storm venturing so near Europe felt much too close for comfort, too soon. And so did the two destructive tornadoes that struck in the following months. I didn't welcome those storms, but I did feel as if I was really living. Paying attention at last. Experiencing the highs and the lows, the big stuff of life. I was, in fact, having a ball. It was like a physical manifestation of the emotional see-saw – like joy following sadness, you appreciate the calms that follow extreme storms so much more than endless days of easy conditions. Rather than cursing a lack of wind, I learned to be grateful for blissful days sunbathing as *Isean*'s engine did all the work.

Those calmer times were spent drifting in a meditative state. Friends back home told me how they desperately struggled to carve out a little chink of space for themselves. Trying to practise mindfulness, they said. It was hard, in lives full of people and stuff, to empty minds whizzing with schedules and tasks. To find the time. I had this in abundance. I had my own mindfulness. Staring at the water or the sky on calm days, my eyes filled with the scale of it, my mind quiet with the peace of it. Often there was nothing but the soothing whoosh of waves and the wind in the sails, the call of birds, *Isean* creaking. I'd be lost in the horizon, all sense of perspective gone, as something caught my eye – a ship ahead, I'd better change course. Oh. No. It's a gull. I paid attention to the far as well as the near, for signs of life – white spray, the blow of air that indicated a whale in the distance. Once you know what to look for, you see more. The coastline was interesting, but it was the sea that really held me, the ever-changing colour and energy. A little line of surf off in the distance – uncharted rocks, watch out. The flotsam floating, planks passing, bottles bobbing. Countless sunsets – that orange ball sinking in the west, usually as I was racing into shelter before dark. '*Boa noite*, old friend, *amanhã*!' Sometimes I'd jump up and down, music blasting, joy spilling over in a mad fit of dancing. Splendidly alone. How could I be this lucky? Sometimes I'd catastrophise – what would I do if my rudder came off? I thought of waterspouts, raging tornadoes whirling across the sea. What would I do? Would I harness on? Go down with *Isean*? I'd hope for the best. I'd imagine the unimaginable. I often pictured a scene described to me by a Moken friend, Hook, a sea nomad hunting on Thailand's Andaman Sea, during the 2004 tsunami. A flat sea, he said. A white wave coming, so big he thought it was a ship. He angled across it, up and over, while fishing boats were tossed around like toys. I shuddered on flat-calm days at the thought of that. I'd stare at postcard skies, little fluffy clouds, a gull hovering, the sun hanging as though someone had placed it just so. A horizon so perfect, I'd picture myself colliding, sailing into a painting on a wall, like Truman.

Often it was less a calm meditation and more of a slog. From Peniche, we were up and off at 6.30 a.m., a strong coffee and slippers on, fifty miles and no sleep till Lisbon. We were blessed with wind on the beam, but exhaustingly, infuriatingly, in the final few hours it was back in front, making for the most gruelling sail for weeks. Upon arrival, though, what reward – in Lisbon we finally shook off the fog. To celebrate this milestone, I had a holiday. I decided to chance one of the tiny marinas the pilot books tell you are only for local boats. *Isean*'s so small I figured they'd find us a space. In we went, the Doca de Belém marina – right beside the imposing *Padrão dos Descobrimentos*, a beautiful ornate monument to Portugal's age of discovery. To my mind, Portugal's greatest discovery was made right there at home in 1837 when the family-owned Pastéis de Belém started making the finest pastries in the world, *pastéis de nata*. In Belém, I was right in the heart of the custard tart. I did what sailors do in cities. I skipped the museums and found the company of other sailors. I sailed someone's drunken boat into the city at night, into the lights and noise of the metropolis, past cranes that scarred a purple sky. We spilled into the throng of pubs and clubs. I tumbled tipsily down Bairro Alto's steep streets, smoking cigarettes and kissing inappropriate men, drank cocktails, went clubbing, walked the handsome River Tagus back to *Isean* at dawn. New friends taught me the Lisboa hangover cure in tiny *ginjinha* bars – standing room only – where they ask no questions and pour you a strong *ginja*. They took me across the river to the hauntingly lovely old industrial district of Almada

and we wandered wastelands dreaming about buying amphibi-
ous dredgers and building ports. Then I sobered up and off I
went, back with my girl, heading south in the sunshine for the
Algarve. In Sines I was joined once again by Cat, who had a
knack for turning up when she was most needed. We had a long
slog ahead, seventy miles to round the notoriously lively Cabo
de São Vicente. What this cape lacked in fog it made up for in
wind, the sea white with Aeolus's horses galloping to welcome
us. I was especially glad to have Cat on the helm as I struggled
with the multitudes of problems that always wait for high winds
before presenting themselves. We turned up into the Algarve
and everything quietened down except us. We were whooping
for joy. I'd made it down the Atlantic coast! Safe from those terrifying winter storms! Soon, all the stress of choppy seas was a
distant memory as we cruised past intriguing little caves in flat
waters, removing layers and looking for sun lotion like a couple
of holidaymakers.

*Wheesht! A thousand miles and here we are. Sahara sand on my win-
dows. Time to stop. Not that I need to. I could keep going. I've been
much farther, with others. She needs to stop, though. It's hard for them
that do it alone. Without their own kind, that is. She's not alone. It's the
two of us. It's us, we, our journey. 'We arrived,' she'll say. 'Me and her.
Isean and I.' Not that you'd know, to listen to the fawning. People blowing smoke up her rear. 'You came all the way on this LITTLE boat?'
Haud yer wheeesht! She corrects them, mind you. I love her for that.
'Little but strong,' she says, patting my hatch. 'She got me here. I just
clung on.'*

*She talks to me. Sometimes too much, like the barnacles on my hull
with their endless crackling, now her chatter too. Solo sailors are this way.
I talk to her too, mind. When I'm not happy. When she's put us on a bad
course — and she does this too often — my hull thuds the heavy waves, my
sails luff in complaint. When she gets the anchor wrong, my chain drags*

and rumbles. I nudge her awake. She should know better by now. When we're in a rough anchorage, I groan as I roll in the swell. And she has the cheek to complain! Can't sleep, she says, for my noise! Wheesht! She oughtn't to sleep in such a badly chosen spot!

I let her know when she gets it right. With the wind and a following sea. Then she knows me at my best. Me and the sea, singing in time. When she chooses a nice safe spot. We both get rest then. She dives our anchor, sees it set, leaves me, at peace with the fish and the birds. Off she goes. And when she comes back! Wheesht! The noise! Thud! A tumble of enthusiasm in the quiet bay, like a child with things she's found. But I smell her before I hear her! A musty animal scent, grassy and warm, from roaming the land. Usually, it's just us in these places. In a moonlit bay, we stay. She and I swaying under the starry Plough. She's grown on me, this one. Like the barnacles but more welcome. I've seen her grow on herself too, this little sister of mine.

8.

By the time I found my winter home, I was exhausted. Cat had left and I'd been sailing hard in bad weather. I'd injured my back, *Isean*'s engine had been overworked – we were both in need of rest when we limped into the tiny Portuguese fishing village of Culatra. This raggle-taggle of fishermen's huts and low cottages sits atop a spit of sand and samphire in the Atlantic, a barrier between the ocean and mainland Algarve. We turned up in the lagoon – the Ria Formosa – at the end of November, surfing in the narrow entrance on big rolling waves. I held my nerve – and my bad back – as we were carried fast towards jagged rocks on one side and concrete armour blocks on the other. Like white-water rafting we could do without. A big relief to get in safe. I tied up on Culatra's rough old cement dock, strewn with piles of nets waiting to catapult the unwary into the sea, and I didn't move for two days. I took in my surroundings as the sun dropped and lights blinked on around the wooden huts above. It was the sort of one-horse town my gran would have loved, what Maw Joss called rough and ready. A few old men with a handful of teeth between them, spitting and shuffling in dressing gowns and slippers; a fishing boat unloading someone's new fridge on the shore. My own slippers were crossed in the air as I slumped back in my cockpit, untangling my hand line amongst fisher-men mending their nets. A friendly youngster came over and welcomed me into the gang with the gift of a squid jig. Like my most exciting day in primary school. I had a bright-red plastic fireman's helmet from a weekend trip to Glasgow's Kelvin Hall and someone – not me! – set off the fire alarm. As we filed into the playground the fire brigade turned up! There I was, thrilled in my hat as they waved down at me. I was almost as happy to be accepted by the Culatra fishermen. One of them brought me a bucket of oysters. I devoured them and the next morning found the bucket refilled, plus a decorative conch shell, that had been left in the cockpit as I slept. Somewhat belatedly, I realised that this token was more of a proposal than an ordinary gift; a series of quaint scenarios followed, with lots of mime and smiling, a focus on my ring finger. An awkward start.

I finally made it off *Isean* and waded through sand dunes to some random paving blocks that eventually turned into a rough path. There were a couple of tascas serving beers and a tiny shop. I followed the path all the way over to the Atlantic side. Beyond a scattering of shacks, the place was entirely empty and completely flat, pelicans flying overhead. A prairie sandscape; no trees, just driftwood and aromatics, chamomile, pungent yellow curry plants and salty samphire. Tumbleweed. The Desperado vibe was strong. Beyond a bridge, the rumbling sound of surf. Although I knew what to expect, the sight still made my jaw drop. One of those endless unspoiled white beaches I'd seen from the sea: a huge runway of sand, miles of it, soft and silky and stretching out of sight. Not a soul there. The sun sinking into the water accompanied by stray dogs howling in the dunes. I had been intending to sail farther east for winter. But I knew a good thing when I saw it. I messaged friends and family. 'I'm home.'

It was December. I'd been sailing constantly for six months. Of all the places I'd found on the way, Culatra was the most suited to my slow pace and scruffy style – no one would bat an eyelid at me. The ideal halfway home. After a couple of weeks acclimatising, *Isean* and I followed the lagoon's winding channel through the mudflats to Olhão, a quirky gem of a town founded by rebel fishermen and now colonised by artists. After Culatra it felt impossibly cosmopolitan, all tasteful Christmas decorations and softly lit shop windows. A nice manageable size. Then I found my way up to the main road on the outskirts, where the cars whizzed and trucks thundered, sirens wailing and horns honking, everything so loud and fast! I weaved my way over to a massive, brutal hypermarket and stood outside blinking up. It had been several months since I'd last been in such a big store – maybe in France. Since then it had mainly been small shops near the coast. I'd drop anchor, row in to get supplies. On return I'd stand looking out at *Isean*, this little boat weirdly alone at sea, the big horizon behind. In those moments even I would think, 'What a strange way to live.' I'd load up my dinghy, walkers staring at me, wild-haired and barefoot; this strange little sea urchin disappearing off into the winter sea alone. Those grocery trips had been disorientating enough, forcing me into shoes and across roads. Here was another world entirely – one I'd forgotten. I wandered slowly around the aisles, stupefied at the colour and sparkle, staring at rows of products: shrink-wrapped fruit among baubles and glitter, plastic toys rattling and buzzing and beeping. The constant stimulation: strip lighting, a looping Christmas playlist and tannoy announcements, children screaming. The overwhelming frantic nature of consumerism at that scale.

The longer I spent at sea, the more waste dismayed me. I had always been bothered by the unnecessary extravagance of every-day products (mini-cheesecakes sold in ceramic ramekins – why?), but as my lifestyle simplified, that disconnect increased. Sometimes I would stare at something as simple as the plastic cap from my milk carton or a perfectly designed little tin or bottle and think about how clever it all is; the ingenuity and energy it took to make these things; the madness of their single use, the energy required for their disposal. I wandered around the aisles, with all their arrows and displays designed to encourage spending. A hyper-reality. It can't be good for us. I remembered that time when too much choice in a sandwich shop had been enough to spark anxiety. But while choice can be overwhelming, we still want it, and if we all want choice, it adds up to a hell of a lot of stuff. Now, after making do with a limited range and expensive products in small shops, I was undeniably delighted to find favourite brands of tinned tomatoes and plant milk, toothpaste and conditioner – and all so affordable!

It's strangely illogical that when you're away, homogeneous products speak of home: the familiarity of the packaging, the reliable textures and flavours. I found I wasn't only craving the food I ate as an adult, though. My tastes went to an earlier time. Suddenly, I was back at our kitchen table after school, smothering toast in Lurpak before my mum caught me filling up ahead of dinner. In front of *Bewitched* or *Alice* at 5 p.m. with Sports Mixtures. A Saturday afternoon spooning tinned beans on white toast, topped with melted cheese. (Cheesy Beanos: a recipe from *Viz*. You're welcome.) I wanted things I hadn't eaten in decades, roamed those hypermarkets buying comfort in chocolate and Cheddar. I don't think I was homesick, but I was reflective. I had left old habits behind, along with the income that paid for them. I'd travelled quite far from the person I'd been, the life I'd built as an adult, and I wasn't sure what would replace it. On that weirdly slow rush south, my thoughts had always been on the next step; on harbours, conditions, weather, how I was doing for time. I hadn't thought about the destination, much less the *why*. Or the *what then*. That question everyone had asked, to which I had no answer. Now, the voyage south was done. My daily purpose gone. I had time to think. Who am I now? What am I doing? There was also the matter of *where am I*, given the entirely unexpected prospect of a winter in Portugal. I embraced it. This long slab of a country surrounded on all sides but Atlantic by effervescent Spain. I was struck by its rhythm and culture, so different from its neighbour. With a little time and effort, I would make some very slow progress in Portuguese, a language that sounded Russian to me. I had a need to make contact, to reach people with words, however faltering. The language may seem harsher than mellifluous Spanish, but the people are quieter by nature, gentler. Modest. There's a kindness there. It takes time to get to know them, but there's such warmth when you do. I grew to love Portugal, an unassuming place that's all feeling, where nostalgia is practically meta. It suited me. I can feel yearning in the simple act of folding my quilt in the morning, clinging to the warmth it retains from my body as I lay on *Isean*, watching a soft sunrise flicker around the cabin. These things we are left with, small details that swell your heart and mean the whole world.

I was alone and it was almost Christmas. I was forced to think about that – to act or to decide on inaction. My family were not big Christmas consumers. When we were kids it was a big deal – I remember the year I got a bike – but once we'd grown up, we dispensed with the pressure of presents; no one cared about decorations or dead trees. My dad was unconcerned, so I had decided to stay with *Isean*. I wasn't worried, was in fact quite excited about the novelty of having Christmas alone for the first time. So it was a shock when I realised I was lonely. There was an inescapable build-up, in the atmosphere around me, in people's cheery travel posts online, the emphasis on family and friends, on plans and parties. Once I'd finally noticed I was sad, I acted to better look after myself. I decided to celebrate with a relatively traditional Christmas dinner, made outside on the barbecue I usually ignored. If nothing else, it would be a fun experiment. I bought a plump little chicken, found cloves to make bread sauce, sourced a starter – carabinero prawns, glistening scarlet, like rubies gift-wrapped in paper. On Christmas morning I sailed – the only boat at sea – then anchored by sandy

Culatra. I prepped vegetables as the sun danced around the saloon, the bird roasting in a bubbling bath of garlic and herbs, butter and white wine. The radio spoke of home. I lifted the lid to find the chicken beautifully browned and spitting. I had a swim, my playlist – Otis Redding, 'Merry Christmas Baby' – ringing cheerfully across the water. The potatoes roasted perfectly. I had bread sauce. A glass of Chablis. A triumph, I told friends and family on the phone. Then I drifted off to sleep, *Isean* gently swaying, me nicely tipsy.

In the new year I joined the local swimming pool – hot showers! – began my Portuguese classes and found myself in an enviable position. Just before Christmas, as a storm had been building, I'd helped Rui, a local guy struggling to shift his tiny sailing boat. He thanked me by bagging me an incredible gift – a much-coveted free mooring on the inside of the breakwater. *Isean* became the only foreign boat to penetrate Olhão harbour, a prime position below the bustling markets. Two huge bazaars, one full of fresh fruit, vegetables and herbs, butchers, local wines and honeys, pulses and grains; the other dedicated to a dizzying variety of fish and shellfish caught in the Ria Formosa and the ocean beyond. On a Saturday, the market swelled and spilled colourfully onto the streets as growers came down from the mountains with their produce. Market day was a social event, the whole town gathered for shopping and lunch, friends pointing to this week's cheapest strawberries and freshest herbs. I spent an average twelve pounds a week and ate very well. I'd been experimenting with food on the trip, making things I'd previously bought. When you're twenty nautical miles from the nearest shop, it's a joy how easily you can knock up a soft, yielding flatbread to wrap around a fried egg. I made yogurt, tried sun-drying tomatoes (better in summer); I considered trailing a tub of cream for the sea to churn into butter (still awaiting trials). What I did buy was made to last. I found the ultimate store-cupboard ingredient in salted cod, big chunks of it kept in the bow, turned into a warming brandade. Then necessity found me filleting and salting a wide range of round and flat fish, after being conned into buying a wily Culatra fisherman's whole catch. I posted an image online and a sharp-eyed fish chef in Penzance alerted me to weever fish lurking in the haul, toxic spines still flattened along their backs. I separated a few chunks of white meaty flesh well away from the bones. Delicious, but not worth the risk. People romanticise buying direct from fishermen – such an authentic experience! Authenticity is overrated.

January temperatures were dropping and I was unprepared. My treasured slippers from Antoine and Nicole in Brittany made up the entirety of my winter wardrobe. I had no heating. I eked out whatever heat I could generate. I'd shower at the public pool, then come home clean and warm to the bones, watch the sun setting over the Ria Formosa. The steamy heat from cooking kept the boat warm through dinner, then the inevitable decline began. Around 9 p.m. I'd wonder if it was too early to go to bed. That was a bit miserable. Being cold in the evening makes you feel sad-alone rather than adventurous-alone. In these early weeks in Olhão, a laundry trip could be the highlight of my evening, for its heating, power sockets and fast broadband. Always on a mission to minimise energy use, I followed my own ethical code when it came to power someone else was paying for. I left ice blocks in supermarket freezers, ready for collection with the following day's shopping. But so much of what we refrigerate – cheese and yogurt, cured meats, butter – keeps perfectly well without. When I finally got heating, my chillbox gravitated outside. Our grandparents' pantries made more sense than cooling down appliances in the middle of heated kitchens. It's upside down. I imagine designers and architects are already using tech that incorporates ambient temperature and natural resources. I became obsessed: water warmed in the sun before boiling, dishes washed in sea water, surplus heat from grilling toast heating the kettle. I was out-dadding my dad. What a fiction it is that we won't adapt. I took real pleasure in my frugality. It's easier when it's driven by choice. The longer my money lasted, the longer I'd be at sea, and there was nothing as motivating as that. I got a buzz out of spending so little – usually around forty pounds a week, much of it on the expensive luxury of plant milk. All this opportunistic scrimping and rule-bending was reminiscent of time spent with my gran. I'm not saying Maw Joss was Fagin – she didn't send us out thieving. Although she would make us 'skip our fare' on trains and ferries. 'My gran's got my ticket,' Lorraine and I were required to shout as we flew down the ramp of the Caledonian MacBrayne ferry. She rewarded us with the price of the fare (and won it back from us at poker). Thanks to her, I was well suited to all the mending, scrimping and reusing, the scouting for energy. And once you've lived this way, it's hard to break the habit. I can't pass a public water tap without checking if it works, can't see a plug socket without mentally mapping it for future use.

Over the weeks, I made *Isean* more habitable. I created a 'lamp' out of a fish grill and fairy lights, hung canvas shelves and treated myself to cushions. Such a homemaker! Then something life-changing happened. I bought a mini wood-burner. Such a clever design – about the size of a shoebox, cast iron, on a base, mounted on the wall. Now I wasn't eyeing my quilt in the evening. I had a new ritual. As the sun disappeared with its warmth, I'd set this tiny fire, paper and twigs and a few lumps of charcoal. Almost immediately, the crackle started, the boat at once cosy. There was just enough room on the top for a casserole pot, vegetables slow-cooking with beans and spices as I sat doing my Portuguese homework. A new kind of joy. I even invited friends over. For I'd made friends now. There was a mix of those who spoke English – the international community of artists who largely made up my Portuguese class – and locals who endured my halting attempts at the language, kind oyster farmers, patiently chatting to me about the *vento forte* out at the *viveiros de ostras*. ('She's obsessed with the wind at the oyster farms,' they must have thought.) I had local friends and those who had settled from former Portuguese colonies – Pedro, a Rastafarian from the Cape Verde Islands who found me inexplicable. 'Impossible to control,' he said, shaking his head at my preference for sailing off alone instead of attending dinners. Best of all I liked to sit at Salvo's kitchen table. An elegant woman from Guinea-Bissau, she was in her seventies, immaculately put together – make-up, earrings, a little hat – full of life and humour, her eyes brown and bright and shining. Her daughter Florbela and I would listen as she reminisced, telling the most wonderful stories from her childhood: the time her father turned to find a tiger in mid-air, claws outstretched, and shot as it lunged at him. How her mother was unafraid of the poisonous snakes in the garden when she was pregnant, for they never attacked a woman with child.

In late January, my dad came, proud of his wayward daughter who had sailed all the way to Portugal on her little boat. Almost eighty, he sported a rucksack like a backpacker on a gap year. I was surprised he wasn't carting his favoured pigskin suitcase – my mum was always dissolving in red-faced laughter at his Edwardian tastes. He stayed with Salvo and Florbela, telling stories and singing, taken hard and fast to their hearts. I wish I'd known my dad when he was a kid. His gang would have been the best gang. At around twelve, he used to bunk off school to wander round Glasgow's Kelvingrove art gallery and museum, staring at paintings and stuffed animals, lost among 'tigers and bears an' wee craturs'. He'd gawp at the giant Asian elephant, a bullet hole still visible in the poor beast's head. He loved the learned atmosphere up there. 'Aye,' he exclaims, remembering how he'd join art students drawing in front of a cage. 'I felt great.' He flew out of school at fifteen, off to work on the 'ferm' with Clydesdale horses, 'big gentle beasts', and he continued with his self-education; he's as well-read as anyone I know. He always has several books going at once; a necessity, he says, because finishing one is like 'losing a friend'.

I would come and find him reading up on Salvo's rooftop and drag him off to the Ria Formosa, where he joined in on a plastic clear-up, grinning and knee-deep in mud. We went kayaking. We ate out and spent cosy nights on board *Isean*, making *caldo verde* and *caldeiradas* by the fire, candlelight and Paul Robeson playing. We took a ferry, the skipper insisting Sam join the men in the wheelhouse – not me, a mere girl. He told them I had sailed there from England, which was more than he could do. He admires strength in women, my dad, a quality he cherished in my mum. Perhaps growing up with four sisters encouraged his progressive outlook. Martha, he said, could beat him at running and fighting. Margaret was the fearsome debater. Nan the top cyclist. Violet, the baby, was the timid one who grew into the family's fiercest protector. He looked after us when my mum went to the women's peace camp at Greenham Common, when she went to work and later, when David and I were teenagers, to study nursing. I missed her but loved his cooking: mash loaded with cheese and onion – Samuel Supresey, he called it – and the surprise breakfast before school one day, the table laden with pastries and cakes. He made a point of supporting my mum in small ways too, getting up from the table to do the dishes as his father Edgar looked on in disapproval, jaw jutting. 'Christ, sir, that's weemin's work!' My dad backed me in whatever I decided to do. It was incredibly special to show him where I'd got to. We took *Isean* the short hop to Culatra, where he stood in that big

Atlantic Ocean, brogues discarded on the sand, moleskin 'breeks' rolled up, away from the biting cold of a Scottish January. He looked for all the world like a happy six-year-old, paddling in the big blue. How the sight swelled my heart.

I was in the Ria Formosa for over four months, delayed by five weeks of exceptionally bad weather. Two tornadoes wreaked havoc just five miles from where *Isean* and I clung to Olhão's harbour. But that time wasn't wasted – what time is? I had a nice routine, I was safe and I became ever fonder of that little town and its people. I took in all the tiny things that add up to a sense of belonging in a place: the chimneys adorned by storks, men digging for *conquilhas* and the scent of curry plants on the breeze. The town's electrical wiring swinging precariously from rooftop to rooftop. And the daily encounters that made me feel part of something. A *bom dia* from the bright-eyed girl who made my morning *galão*; the chatty baker who sold delicious bread, still warm and elastic from the oven; the sullen woman who dispensed paper in the public loos. The human geography that makes up our emotional landscapes. I wonder how many of these familiar faces we remember as we move through life, the expressions of characters we never get to know, forever imprinted in our minds. How these little things draw you in. How easily you put down roots. Friends didn't want me to leave and I started to feel the same, hearing of summer barbecues, the flowers that flourish on a certain path, yearning to be part of it all. It's bitter-sweet, knowing that you will leave. I would come to know it well, this longing to stay. Things are good here. I have friends. A base. Why leave? Where could be better? There's the apprehension of going back to sea, a harbour rot that even experienced sailors feel. It's always wrong. I'm always happy when I do leave. Always fast back to being in love with *Isean*, with the sea and the journey. There are great people everywhere, ideal circumstances all over the place, so many wonderful places to feel at home. I did have a catch in the throat as I left the Ria Formosa, though, quietly and up early to avoid goodbyes. In Portuguese, *saudade* is a longing for and acceptance of that which is gone – expressed in the mournful minor keys of its fado music, and in its people, not afraid to show regret. One friend, I saw him at sea, clasping his heart on the morning I sailed away – *tenho saudades tuas*. Beautiful people, I miss them too.

9.

Rising up ahead, the Pillars of Heracles. Africa's mighty Jebel Musa to the south, the Rock of Gibraltar to the north. We'd sailed a hundred miles from Olhão, past the bordering Guadiana river, where the Portuguese clock rings one time and the Spanish responds with another. *Isean* and I passed west to east through the narrow strait that lies between two continents, between African mountains and macaque monkeys. We were riding high, speeding along on the strong currents that flow like a conveyor belt between the Atlantic Ocean and the Mediterranean Sea. The haze was clearing – the Rock is often capped by clouds that enclose this British crown colony in a microclimate of authentic drizzle – and I was reeling at my first glimpse of Africa. Unbelievably yet unmistakably Morocco, just seven nautical miles away; so close you'd smell it if the wind turned. But I'd rather it didn't. The Levant often blows through here, a strong easterly, but, for once, we had luck – a nice steady north-westerly helping us along with the tide. We were on a broad reach, a lovely point of sail that levels out the boat and allows you to relax and enjoy the journey. And I couldn't have been more excited about this passage, about what I might see. It was the end of April and, like us, the bluefin tuna would be leaving the Atlantic and migrating through the strait for the Mediterranean, the females full of eggs and looking to spawn.

We had set off after a night on anchor in the little fishing town of Barbate, settled on the approach to the strait and the tuna's migratory route. It's no surprise that bluefin – or as locals have it, *pata negra* of the sea – has been economically crucial to this region for thousands of years. The Romans produced coins in neighbouring Cádiz depicting the once bountiful fish. Like the tuna, we'd need to avoid getting caught in the *almadraba*, a complex chamber system of trap nets pioneered by those intrepid sailors the Phoenicians, and still employed by local fisheries. I didn't need a net in my prop and another major passage blighted with engine problems. But I was less interested in the bluefins' human hunters than their other top predator – the endangered orcas that prey on them. A small pod pursues the tuna here each spring. With eyes wide open, I set off, after reading the almanac. 'To minimise the risk of collision with whales,' it cautioned, speed must be reduced 'and a good lookout kept'. Giants are here. Deep-diving sperm whales and baleens – fin whales that can reach three times *Isean*'s length. Awe-inspiring and daunting in equal measure. I hadn't seriously considered colliding with whales, but I was struck by the thought of it, and of the stress they must endure, hunting amongst noisy ships and high-speed vessels using radar. A shark passed us by, its fin cutting a thrillingly distinctive straight line through the water; a dolphin joined us – never not joyful; but if there was anything else, I didn't see it, probably because I was staring at the coast of Africa and that was epic enough. We passed Tarifa, Spain's wind hotspot, where the kitesurfers get their mental and literal highs from the strong winds funnelling through the strait. Sure enough, the breeze picked up and so did we. By the time we turned north into the Bay of Gibraltar, we were flying on a close reach, heeling over, exceeding six and a half knots in the gusts. So exciting. Fancy superyachts cruised past, but no one was as high as me that day – not even the kitesurfers winging through the air back around the corner. I'd been apprehensive about coming into the Mediterranean, but I was suddenly ecstatic to be there. Another milestone passed – I smiled from ear to ear with pride. Looking at the majestic edge of Africa was a just reward, I thought, for having managed to sail my little boat all the way there. But the thing about pride? After it, always – always – a fall.

May Day. The first of May and my worst storm at sea. We'd left La Linea well stocked up. I'd made several giddy trips across the Spanish border to a well-known Yorkshire supermarket in Gibraltar. A strange sensation, passing the British bobbies and red postboxes, the *Daily Mail*s and Union Jacks; the patriotic pride, as distinctive as the smell of British bangers in the air. Like Britain in the fifties maybe, more English than England. For my part, I was happily wheeling a small suitcase of comfort food; at the top, a stack of that sweet milk chocolate originally made by nice Quakers in Bournville. *Isean*'s modest storage space was now bulging with beans and cheese. Dairy Milk soon became essential on board, added to the visitors' bring list along with teabags. It was destined to fulfil a specific role I'd sooner not have needed – storm chocolate. We'd set off from Gibraltar. I had planned to sail to Morocco, so close it was technically a breeze, but the sea felt sloppy and steep, different from the Atlantic, and it unnerved me. A dolphin accompanied me for a couple of miles, cutting through those big waves, and I felt so jealous – how perfectly adapted it was in rough seas. I was put off by the prospect of seven miles of heavy pummelling. For the first time ever, I turned back. Africa could wait – she's still waiting, in fact.

We meandered round the Spanish coast in calmer seas. I tied up for the night in Estepona, smiling at the coincidence of landing there. This little town had been the site of our family's first foreign holiday – a surprise package trip to Spain in the eighties. My mum had taken a look at my dad, up on the roof of the house, working in torrential rain for weeks.

He needed a break, she'd decided. Off she'd gone with the money they'd scrimped for building materials, then she came back and told Sam the plan. I must have been about thirteen. They told my brother David and me the night before we went. Two weeks off school in October. The best thing that had ever happened. I don't remember the sea on that holiday; mine were mainly stray kittens and food-based memories. I'd been allowed chicken and chips every night. And strawberries and cream – with a sparkler in it! On this visit, I was more keen to fill up on water and leave before being charged for a night on the harbour wall. We headed up the coast, where the sea was pleasantly flat but the air heavy and moist, the sky teeming with rain clouds – the kind of moody weather that often accompanies the shoulder seasons of autumn and spring. We passed Fuengirola, a safe harbour I should have stopped in, but I was keen to make progress, inching up the coast to Benidorm to cross for the Balearic Islands, before July's extortionate mooring costs hit. Ahead, dark cumulonimbus clouds were piling up over the Montes de Málaga, Andalucía's stunning mountain range. I stared in awe, appreciating the unreal light as tall black clouds bowled dramatically towards us. The first thing I thought to do was take a picture. The second thought, following closely behind – reef! I should reduce my sails. Too late. The storm hit us, a squall as sudden as it was furious. The noise! Gusts screeched like the getaway car on a bank heist. Thunder rumbled and lightning cracked. The sea was black, reflecting an incandescent sky, and torrential rain swept sideways across the surface of the water. I could no longer see the coast; the whole scene looked and sounded disconcertingly like mid-ocean. You don't have a lot of time to think in this situation, but you have plenty of time to feel. One feeling dominated. Terror.

Wind powered up the sails and we sped off. The dinghy,

trailing behind, flipped and its floor flew into the distance. I was in complete panic and *Isean* seemed equally frightened, like a wild thing, out of control and swerving crazily. We were tipped on our side, the left gunwale underwater, waves washing over the side. In no time, without a life jacket or safety harness, I was merely clinging on. When things go badly wrong on a boat, you want to hide but you have to act. No one else can help you. You overcome fear because the alternative is worse, and you find a physical strength fuelled by adrenaline and desperation. *Isean* powered up to the wind as I fought to steer off and furl in her foresail, inch by inch, desperate to take the power out. But the line jammed. I was aghast. Now I had to get to the bow. Our world was upside down, the starboard deck high in the air. I crawled along it, whipped painfully by a merciless wind that lashed me with stinging wet ropes. It was chaos, sails flapping, ropes flying, the forestay violently rattling. Inside, I would discover, was worse: a formless pile of food and oil, equipment and clothes, solids and liquids intermingled, all atoms fighting for space. Eventually, arms aching, hands throbbing in pain, I wrestled both sails away, felt the boat even out and we turned downwind. The gusts screeched from behind, still heart-poundingly strong, but I was back in control. I got the engine on and motored out to sea for space. There was plenty. We were totally alone. No one else was stupid enough to be out there. Heading away from the comfort of land in a storm is without a doubt the loneliest feeling in the world. All you want is a safe harbour, other boats, other people, but what you need is sea space. As quickly as it had come, the squall passed. I apologised to *Isean* and started to cry. I felt extremely stupid and utterly alone. I had no right to be out here, putting myself and my boat in such danger. It was completely irresponsible. I'd been lucky. *Isean*'s substantial weight and stability had kept us safe. But, even in those moments of shock and remorse, I knew I would recover myself. My mistake had been so obvious, the consequences so terrifying, I wouldn't repeat it. It was another learning experience. I'd be off again first thing in the morning, but now it was time to stop. I sniffed pathetically all the way back to Fuengirola. An hour later, feeling very sorry for myself, we limped into the little port and dropped anchor in a flat-calm sea. People strolled the promenade with ice creams and sunbathed on loungers. The sun shone as if nothing had happened, mocking me. Still trembling an hour later, I went to bed with a cup of tea and a massive bar of chocolate. My second day in the Med and a perfect introduction to conditions there.

I did not know you could miss an ocean. A week in and I was longing for the Atlantic, its big westerly swell, the rhythm of tides, predictable winds. If the sea is a teacher, we were in a very different school now, with new patterns and hazards to learn. Most people think of the Med as the picture-postcard sea of their holidays, all flat blues glistening in the sun. Smaller than an ocean, surely more manageable, and with barely any tide – one less thing to worry about. Sailors know a different sea. Mediterranean waves are ruled by other beasts. Aeolus knew them, thanks to Zeus. This keeper of the winds was king of floating Aeolia, the ancient Greeks said. As a parting gift, he gave Odysseus a bag containing all the violent storm winds, casting just the Zephyr, a fair westerly to blow him home to lovely Ithaca. Odysseus's mistrusting and greedy crew opened the bag, thinking it held untold riches, and in the process unleashed those terrible winds, galloping the ship back to Aeolus's shore. Nightmare. (This is why it's better to sail solo.) As with the Solent's tides, it won't do to go against these winds: the Levant, Poniente, Sirocco, Mistral, Tramontane, Bora, Meltemi, each with its own ferocious character.

Those winds are strong but usually forecast. More of a problem are the unpredictable localised winds that rush out of nowhere, like a mugging at sixty knots, then veer from one direction to another. The thing is all the land. It's always the land that makes you wary at sea. You see white water ahead, look around for culprits – headlands, gaps in the hills. There we go, those beautiful sheer-faced mountains, ideal for the wind to rush down, gathering speed. And all that earth everywhere, baking under the hot Mediterranean sun, sending nice warm air off and up to eventually meet you, whistling and weaponised in some dark corner, funnelling terrifyingly up estuaries, bending and swerving forcefully around bays. You just have to deal with it, run for shelter, reduce sails, cry, swear, whatever gets you through.

The sea made me angrier than the wind, though. It was a mess. Sailing around the coast of Spain, it would often start off well enough, calm in the mornings, but by the afternoon the wind would whip it into an onslaught of steep, uncomfortable waves that had me swearing by teatime. It felt heavy, obstinate, ungraceful somehow – mean and small-minded compared to my beloved Atlantic. It wouldn't even exist, the Mediterranean, were it not for the Atlantic. Almost didn't, in fact. It nearly dried up a few million years ago, until the ocean found its way in through the Strait of Gibraltar. That choppy water collapsed my sails in light winds that constantly changed direction. And when they were not changing direction they would change strength – now five knots, now thirty knots, now ten knots. I'd put the sails away in a temper, only to grudgingly pull them out again five minutes later, then back in. The engine was our friend, but it didn't much appreciate the constant bouncing, the prop coming out of the water with a dreadful racket. East of Málaga was not a coastline blessed with shelter either, so I was in a thoroughly bad mood with this capricious sea as we slogged our way through fifty miles of it a day. As I was battered at sea, my friends were pummelled by moody messages.

Smillie's people

SUSE: The sea hates me :(Morning. It's all a mess. Confused.

CAT: Confused? Have you eaten, Smillie?

SUSE: Not me! The sea is confused. Always storms now.
We bust the weather.

SUSE: Phil, is metal tiller dangerous in lightning?

PHIL: No, it's connected to a fibreglass rudder.

PHIL: You're in a lightning storm. Oh god.

CAT: Oh Smillie. Try to eat.

SUSE: I'm cross. I hate sailing. I HATE THE MED.
It's a stupid sea.

SUSE: Hola! 10 miles to go and snowy mountains! OMG I saw
pilot whales and a TURTLE! I'm so happy!

Tossed around in that springtime sea, I was conflicted about whether to stay. I kept thinking back to the Atlantic, to Olhão. I could be happy, I thought, basing myself there, venturing out when I felt like sailing, returning to a safe harbour with friends and hot showers. I was starting to see why proper sailors avoid the Med. Apart from the terrible conditions, I knew it would get horribly busy in summer; that boats were seen primarily as a source of income; that it was a different culture from, say, seafaring Brittany, where you'd be welcomed into a harbour by people who understood how hard the sea can be. I had been unsure about coming in at all, but culturally it was a real draw – I'd never been to Rome or Venice, and those places I had been – the French Riviera, the Amalfi Coast – I longed to visit by sea. And east. Odysseus's sailing ground beckoned – those beautiful Greek islands. In those first days I told myself I could return to Portugal whenever I wanted, but the farther you slog on, the harder it is to turn round.

The day after my little squall, I was off before sunrise, forty-five miles, a gruelling fourteen hours ahead. We left the province of Málaga firmly behind for less developed shores south of Granada. The Maro-Cerro Gordo nature reserve stretched along where the Costa del Sol turns into the Costa Tropical, the cliff tops transformed from Málaga's headache of shining apartment blocks to old Roman towers, pine and carob trees, shy ibex peering from the scrub. And mountains. This was compensation, and then some. Peaks everywhere, the Sierra de Almijara rising to the sky and dropping abruptly to sea. Sailing past the majesty of the white-capped Sierra Nevada marked the moment I really came round to the Med. It felt so epic, viewed from the sea – I loved being small and entirely alone in this wild landscape. Mostly. Off one isolated cliff face I met a young guy on a jet ski. He revved up, circling *Isean* closely as I stood in my bikini. No response to my greeting. Just staring, unsmiling, for far too long, as if contemplating something right beside me. Perhaps it wasn't sinister. Perhaps he was interested in the boat, wondering how I came to be sailing there by myself. Maybe he was simply not thinking, in the way that some men don't, about how intimidating his behaviour was. How it ignited that age-old fear all women have grown up with – regretting how we're dressed, thinking ahead, how can I defend myself? He left suddenly, his machine revving and roaring at speed, in the macho way young men often do. It hadn't been the first time I'd felt uneasy around a man on this trip, and it wouldn't be the last. We shook off the discomfort with a cracking sail, heading north-east to the cove of San Pedro. By the time we'd sailed to Murcia, I was totally sold on the Mediterranean, if not for the sea state and ridiculous wind, for the landscapes. I found myself in the wilderness of the stunning Cabo Tiñoso marine reserve – entirely alone in Cala Cerrada, a perfect little circular bay surrounded by mountains, miles from the nearest habitation. We swayed gently on calm waters to the incongruous soundscape of crashing waves – the acoustics playing it all up to dramatic effect. I was exhausted and blissfully happy. I realised how completely I'd changed when I posted a picture online, expecting everyone to revel in my beautiful isolation, only to hear my dad wonders if I'm safe, out there in the dark, and friends wonder if I'm lonely. 'Yes, I'm safe,' I told him. I didn't tell him how much safer I felt there – hidden in the middle of nowhere – than in a harbour with drunk men outside my boat. I was, I realised, now more at home at sea than anywhere else.

Which is why, soon after, I found myself flying along under the moon at 4 a.m., feeling invincible in a pitch-black Alboran Sea. *Isean* and I were forty miles east of Alicante, equidistant from mainland Spain and the Balearic Islands. The constellations were at their brightest and best, Ursa Major keeping us on course, and I was terrifically excited to be on my first solo night passage offshore. *Isean* was on a beautiful broad reach, in perfect balance with the elements, and I was entirely in tune with her. I was tired – I'd been awake since seven the previous morning – but who needed sleep! We were over halfway to Ibiza, where the water is crystal clear. At 3:15 a.m. I recorded my position in the logbook – 38 12.344′ N 0 26.999′ E – 'Glorious!' Conditions were great, a strong wind behind, big waves pushing us fast, right on course. For once, everything aligned. Then, out of the blue, life, in its habitual way, interrupted with other plans. A radio call on channel 16. The one you dread at sea. 'Mayday Mayday Mayday. Man overboard.' It was Tjoppe and Helena, Swedish friends made in Portugal, now sailing roughly five miles to my west. I could see their boat *Wilma*'s mast light in the distance. They had been pursued, Helena told the coastguard, by a small boat full of men. It had purposely crashed into them and they had been boarded. As this unthinkable news sank in, I changed course towards them, *Isean* speeding up to over six knots as her beam caught the wind that was behind. The Alicante coastguard had launched a rescue boat, but it was several hours away. I would be first on the scene.

Isean was responding well to this emergency, efficient and calm, sailing beautifully. I was a different story, experiencing the sort of fear that takes you out of yourself, making everyday tasks feel alien. I tried to start the engine for extra control, but it took several attempts to turn the key because my hands were shaking so much. My body was all over the place – my heartbeat sprinting, my mind in a dizzying race with my heart. More information came through. They were migrants in distress, eleven men. Only one had made it on board. As the boat bounced off *Wilma*'s high concrete hull, two others had been thrown into the sea. I radioed to tell Tjoppe I was approaching. 'No!' he responded immediately. 'Don't come. It might be bad for you.' I took it in soberly. I was scared. I worried for the safety of my boat. How many people could *Isean* hold? I worried for my own safety – what kind of state would they be in, these men, and what kind of men? I mentally paused. Tjoppe had given me an out. Thinking of my own safety even as he was unsure of their own. My body was brutally, shamelessly honest: a wave of relief rushed over me. But I knew I couldn't take the out. There were people in the water. Another boat could only help. 'I'm still coming,' I told him, sounding braver than I felt. He didn't put me off again. It was typically big of him to try at all. I felt such gratitude, such love, for both of them in those moments.

Isean hadn't hesitated, carrying us fast forward. Their light was getting brighter; we were getting nearer. Twenty minutes later we were there, the air heavy with the scent of petrol, the sea oily black. I drifted too close to the small boat pitching in a heavy swell. The two men were already back aboard amongst the others, some slumped forward, some leaning over the sides. Some, I realised with alarm, were smoking – in this boat awash with petrol. I caught the wind in *Isean*'s sail and quietly sailed off. They shouted angrily in French at *Wilma*'s new passenger – Nigel, he had said to call him – who was now on deck with a blanket and water. The men were seasick and cold. They wanted off that grim dinghy. And who could blame them? They had been at sea for five days, travelling 100 miles from Algeria, and had run out of food and water. Nigel told them the coastguard was coming. Yes, he reassured them several times, definitely the Spanish coastguard.

They had been drifting and desperate, Nigel explained to Helena, when they spotted *Wilma*'s lights. They used the last of their fuel, went full throttle. Helena had wakened to the sound of men screaming, their boat swerving close at speed. They launched themselves into *Wilma* in panic. I thought about that as I sailed in the dark. It could have been *Isean*'s light. They would have boarded us easily. Eleven panicked men. I didn't want to picture it. Suddenly, Helena came back on the radio. 'Get away.' She sounded worried. 'They are coming after you.' I looked back to see the boat heading for me. To my relief, their engine quit. I sailed farther off, feeling anxious and guilty. They must have been at a loss what to do, desperate to get out of the situation they were in. I didn't know what to do either. Nothing felt right. I didn't want to leave in case the situation deteriorated and I was needed. But being there on my accessible little boat was just taunting them. Even if I knew *Isean* could handle the weight of ten extra men (I did not), and even if I was comfortable with that prospect (I was not), these steep seas were not the conditions in which to attempt it. The safest thing was to wait for professional help. Then again, what was safe in the short term might not have been safe for them in the long term. They had left Algeria, where 'illegal exit' was a criminal offence with six months in prison. And it was an increasingly dangerous country for migrants in 2018. Al Jazeera, Associated Press and others told of numerous attacks on migrants, of thousands rounded up by gendarmes and forced at gunpoint into the Sahara Desert. For each person estimated to have died crossing the Mediterranean, two were lost in that vast sea of sand. A dinghy adrift on the water might well have seemed like good odds.

That dinghy had been blown a long way north. There was no phone signal, no land in sight. I doubt Nigel and the others knew where they were. Or who might be coming for them. I heard the helicopter before I saw it and watched its approach with relief – the Spanish coastguard, shining a light, radioing to see if emergency treatment was needed. But what was a welcome sight for us – we're not alone out here – caused them panic. Suddenly the boat took off, only for their engine to splutter to an impotent halt. It was desperately sad to see. Perhaps they didn't believe it was the Spanish coastguard. Or they feared a return to whatever situation they had taken such risks to escape. The helicopter crew decided against an airlift and left. Twice more the guys made for me; twice more they failed. I watched them lurch towards me as I sat there, miserable and apprehensive in the dark. You're very aware, in proximity to humans in a dangerous situation, that you are also in danger. But while our situation was tense, it no longer felt desperate – the coastguard was on its way. I thought of Italy, where the political atmosphere had hardened in response to migration by sea. Migrant rescue calls went unheeded, reports said; rescuers faced arrest for 'trafficking'. I tried to imagine how scared I would feel – how dangerous things would be – if there was no help coming. I wasn't frightened any more. I was exhausted, aching and cold. I sat there for a couple of hours, considering the time added to my onward journey in this sleepless state, the extra risk that brought. I thought about the days – five of them – that these guys had been tossed around on a far less seaworthy boat. I made tea. How could I think of tea at a time like this? I sat there at a distance, selfishly and secretly with my tea, swinging between compassion, anxiety, self-pity and guilt.

With the coming light, things started to improve, as they invariably do with the energy of a new day. I could see the boat clearly now, the men huddled together. Soon after daybreak, I saw it in the distance. The coastguard launch, its cheery red hull bright against the dark sea. The sun rose, casting everything in golden rays. A new dawn if ever there was one. I watched as the boat picked up those men – what relief for them, to get off that fuel-soaked dinghy. Then it approached *Wilma* carefully, both vessels rocking in the swell, a beautiful scene framed by long clouds etched silver. Nigel was transferred across, with a hearty hoot of the horn. The men lined up, touched their hearts. A thank you to Tjoppe and Helena, everyone in tears. Then the coastguard boat was on its way to mainland Spain. And we were bound for the Balearics, *Isean* and I set off first, the Swedes behind on *Wilma*. They offered me a tow I wouldn't take; it would slow them down. Progress was painful. I was beyond tired and the sea was now a sloppy mess. There wasn't enough wind to sail but when I turned on the engine I couldn't bear the noise. With no autopilot, I couldn't leave the helm and fell asleep there for seconds at a time. I hallucinated. Some mad thing about the Queen and jam doughnuts. It was evening before I reached my destination, thirty-six hours awake. In a daze, I almost motored straight into *Wilma*, arrived before me. 'Not another crash,' they said, throwing me a bedtime beer. What a relief it was to anchor, to get inside *Isean*'s welcome little saloon. But even after sleep, the following days felt surreal and distorted. We were in Ibiza. Party island. Surrounded by superyachts with helicopters, rich kids with every conceivable gadget, music blasting and ostentatious wealth on display. Just forty miles and another world from that night. No distance at all, just an insurmountable gulf.

I'd never considered being pursued at sea, but I'd thought about the refugee crisis when I approached the Med. I'd seen the news reports, back in 2015, of the desperation unfolding, the heartbreaking photo of little Alan Kurdi, washed ashore in Turkey, videos of hundreds adrift on that troubled sea. Images that stuck powerfully with me. In the years since, media attention had waned but the crisis had not. In those quiet days when I catastrophised about tsunamis or water-spouts, I also contemplated human disaster, meeting migrants in trouble. I imagined the worst-case scenario — too many panicked people for one small boat to help. What would you do? Advice, as I understood it, was to radio the coastguard, to stand-off rather than to approach. Rescue at sea is a sacred principle — if you can carry it out safely. I pushed the thoughts away. Like a hurricane, you hoped it wouldn't come. I knew of no sailors who had experienced this. It was extremely unlikely to happen on the routes I'd be taking. And it really was a surprise to find migrants so far north of Africa. But migration routes shift and the EU had recently closed the busiest, often pushing people into riskier journeys. A deal with Turkey in 2016 was designed to stem the flow of migrants to Greece, and in 2017 Italy signed a 'Memorandum of Under-standing' with Libya, to intercept people fleeing those shores. By mid-2018, when we were there, according to a UN report,

Spain was a hotspot, fast becoming the primary entry point to Europe. Deaths on that route had almost quadrupled over the previous year. For each day that we'd sailed the Mediterranean, an estimated average of six migrants drowned in its seas.

Figures. News. Reports. Remote and unreal. The reality hits you like a truck. Something physical. A collision of worlds that are closer than you know. It's coming up hard against the uncomfortable truths of the world, your privileged place within it. It's coming up hard against yourself, unedited, in the dark. You hear about people, heroic people – good people – going headlong into risky situations without pause for thought. In the forty minutes it had taken me to get there, I did not feel brave and I did not feel good. I had time enough to fear – and I was a conflicted mess of feelings in the dark. I hadn't hesitated in acting; it's just that my head was giving me trouble on the way. Fear, I suppose – a human, just being. Intrusive, unwelcome thoughts creeping in as I contemplated the scene I might face. 'What kind of men?' I'd thought. Eleven desperate men. Anonymous strangers in the dark. A threat by default, on an off-shore sea. Scary at a distance. But up close, eleven separate individuals, each face loved by someone. Someone's father. Someone's lover. Someone's hero older brother. Every one, someone's special son.

I hadn't liked myself much back there. I had gone, but I hadn't wanted to. I had compassion, but it was conditional. My first thoughts were of my own safety. My overriding feelings were fear and mistrust. That felt horrible. I was no altruist – but this was not news to me. Humans are largely selfish. Sometimes we have to be. You can't help anyone else if you don't look after yourself. I told myself these things, but I still did not feel good. I made peace with myself in the end, surrounded by the super-wealthy, in that parallel universe. I was not a hero, but I wasn't a coward either. Somewhere in the middle. Like most of us, I suppose. I thought about the wisdom of offshore passages alone. Boat lights at night took on a different significance. The world had reminded me I was far from invincible. It's that saying, one that took on currency during the pandemic. It had greater meaning for me out there in the dark. No one is safe until everyone is safe.

I dived down to my anchor, through six metres of water that was so clear I didn't need to go – I could see it had set from the surface. But it's a ritual I love. On the way back, a little school of curious saddled sea bream chased behind me, all blue and glistening silver, their black-striped tails marking them out. They were following me but pretending not to, as they always do. I turned round fast, trying to catch them out; they were faster, darting sideways, looking elsewhere, practically whistling. 'What, us? No, no, we're not interested in you.' I laughed. Sure, sure, and you've not just followed me from thirty metres away. I'm talking to the fish now. But why not? There was no one else there. I came for protection from the strong westerly wind that was forecast. Normally I'd be nervous anchored entirely alone in a storm, no other boats to affirm my choice of shelter. But I no longer needed that. I'd chosen well; tucked into this incredible bay on the eastern shores of Mallorca, I was confident of my decision. And my reward, desolation – sea room, no other boats to drag and swing near me, peace to revel for days in the most stunning anchorage I'd found. There were three empty inlets side by side – Cala Magraner, Cala Pilota, Cala Virgili – long fingers of water pushing deep into the land, little white crescents of sand at the ends, like perfectly manicured nails. Above, on the cliff tops, amongst the bushes, one sign of human interference – a gravel track for the adventurous, the climbers and the hikers. It was miles from anything – not many came, by bike or by foot. Day boats brought snorkelling tourists, but they left as we arrived and, with the winds forecast, wouldn't be back. Gulls gleamed white in the sunshine, soaring and wheeling over cliffs alive with movement – sure-footed goats, hares, chicks nesting. I stood in silence after I anchored, mouth agape, looking around in disbelief at my good fortune.

Floating on the surface, I watched the schools of fish below, listened to the crackling of their noisy lunch on the go. We hung in a cloud around *Isean*, her shadow a gift, bringing relief from the sun. I went down again for a look. I never tire of admiring her below the waterline, her elegant hull suspended as if showcased in mid-air like the *Cutty Sark*. Shoalmates clustered around her shapely bottom – little social schools of dreamfish, all yellow stripes off in one direction; glinting silver threads of needlefish weaving in the shade; dense shoals of dark damselfish, forked tails propelling them first one way, then another. I was still unused to this hypnotic water, so clear it made me laugh in bubbles of delight. I held my breath and dropped, ran my hand along *Isean*'s keel, slimy with seaweed. I swam along the bottom, back up at the rudder. She had some barnacles. I'd have to do some scraping, the closest I get to the daily grind in this, the workplace of a child's finest imagination. I free-dived, a couple of minutes at a time, inspecting the seabed for rocks that a strong gale might push us towards. There were none large enough to worry me. I followed the curves of the sea floor where it bends and bulges, drops into gullies and small ravines, fish nibbling at algae-covered boulders. The sand, white and perfectly formed, a picture of pleasing patterns, like etchings of waves studded with starfish. The whole scene rippled with veins of golden light and shade, a net made of sun gently draped over us. I swam to softly swaying meadows, ribbons of *Posidonia oceanica*, endemic to the Mediterranean, its grass and its lungs. Its long leaves trap floating sediment – I silently thanked them for that insanely clear water. As with the mangrove forests of the tropics and Britain's wetlands and marshes, seagrass offers protection. It absorbs carbon dioxide, filters and oxygenates the water, slows the swell and helps defend the shoreline from storms and erosion – I thanked them too, for the beautiful white beaches. And I floated there in hope.

If you're far from the noise of outboards and other human sounds, you might hear little peals, the meadow's oxygen bubbles bursting, like tiny bells ringing. It is perhaps the noise from these meadows that guides the creatures who call them home. *Posidonia oceanica* provides a sanctuary for the fragile *Hippocampus hippocampus* and *Hippocampus guttulatus* – short- and long-snouted sea horses – that once thrived here and are now rare. In this *cala*, Poseidon's dark leaves grow in thick tangles where the cliffs meet the sea. From above, the water moves in stunning shades: jade, edged by thick forest green, and later, when the sun shifts, azure and midnight blue. Sometimes you see scars where our human things – anchors, chains, propellers, fishing gear – have dragged through the grass, and sometimes those scars don't heal. Back down below, I checked that *Isean*'s chain would not swing in the storm and disturb this ancient garden. After all, there was plenty of room. It was just us there. Back on board for coffee, I was bursting with an overwhelming happiness I had come to know only with *Isean*. I had food to last for days. I had water. I had wine. I wanted nothing more. I watched the sun go down, then I watched the stars appear, one by one. I ate, I drank. I probably smiled in my sleep. And the wind did come, but it did not come to our shores. And neither did anyone else. I rose early, awake with dawn, excited at my surroundings. That first look outside – the wilderness framed by the window, made mine somehow. Swimming, eating, floating; hours spent just staring, listening, in an empty paradise.

Up the cliffs I climbed, admiring *Isean* from above – one white dot in a vast blue sea. I left her and headed inland, clambered over rolling hills. I tramped over sand and gravel, through grassy fields where hares darted. I wandered through cool woods and warm wool barns. I was still up there as the sun started to fall, quietly soaking up forgotten charms of the pastoral: bees buzzing, goat bells clanging, the cooing of doves, the songs of cicadas drummed in stomachs hungry for love. Then I headed back to that idyllic place, its cliffs stained orange as the sun dropped low to the horizon. The water gurgled and echoed as it splashed around the caves. I rowed there, lay in the dinghy staring up. With sunset came goats, brown against the white rocky tops. With one goat came a cruel streak. I saw it! A casual glance down, a back kick and, suddenly, a ball of grey fluff launched into the air, falling, flapping into the water beside me. A gull chick. A hoodlum goat! The fledgling struggled in the swell pushing it towards the rocks. I don't love gulls. I don't like their aggressive ways and cold reptilian eyes. Their call isn't tuneful. And I don't like how they borrow my food only to return it, digested, on top of *Isean*. But as I watched this chick, all scrawny, wet and frightened, I was moved. Enough to foolishly risk my dinghy, paddling into the jagged cave to retrieve it. You would have done the same. It was unbearable, its little head ducking down, its eyes narrowing in fear and its fragile body steeling itself against razor-sharp edges. The sight of a creature struggling brings out my merciful side. The same fly I might violently murder just for landing on me, repeatedly (why are they so provocative?) – if it was drowning, I might also launch an ambitious rescue mission. Playing God, I suppose.

Into the dinghy with the chick, a position mapped into my phone, and back to the boat. '*Isean*, we have company.' I fed it a mix of sardine, yogurt and brown bread. It ate hungrily and pecked me ungratefully. I filled a furry hot-water bottle, put it in the basket with the damp chick and covered the basket with a tea towel. No idea why. Perhaps it was something remembered from my gran – Maw Joss did that to her caged budgies, those poor things stuck in Clydebank instead of the Australian savannah. It's strange that she had caged birds at all. She hated domesticated pets, shunning my cat ('spylt!') but taking us to feed the feral cats in the glen. I guess it was common at the time – humans greedy to own a bit of nature. On the other side of the family, Edgar, my grandfather, kept birds too. My dad sometimes escaped his four sisters to sleep in the 'bird room', he told me. He loved wakening to the canaries' melodies flowing out above his head – 'they wur braw chanters' – and hated to see them caged but couldn't persuade his dad against it. My dad loves birds too, but he loves them free. He once found an injured linnet in a herried nest and nursed it back to health. It perched on the edge of my brother Stephen's cot singing. 'Stephen, a wee baby,' he laughs at the memory, 'reaching up trying to grab it.' I phoned and told him about the helpless thing cowering in the cave. Stupid to risk the dinghy, I confessed, feeling silly. 'Naaaaaw,' he exclaimed, 'yae hud tae help it.' I can see my dad now in his garden, delighted by the goldfinches that come in flashes of red and yellow, awestruck at the elegant flight of the swifts, cheered by the cheeky sparrows he calls speugs – 'Well they're common sparrows, but that's dain them down,' he says. 'I know they're common but I love them!' Whenever I see a gannet, elongated, snowy-white and black-tipped, diving into the sea, I think of my dad, his lips blowing – *whooooo* – at the power and grace. He loves all birds, even scavenging gulls. 'Aye! Ah like their brass neck!'

I was waking up in my own little bird room, with the distinct feeling of being watched. I looked over, half remembering, half dreading. The fledgling's snake eyes! It had poked its head through the towel. We stared at each other, confused. A little spillage on the berth – 'Great,' *Isean* probably thought, 'I'm the only boat in the world to have bird shit on the inside.' Out we went, breakfast in the cockpit, home-made sardine pâté for the chick, a croissant for me. Gulls flew overhead. One swooped past, squawking urgently. I saw the fledgling respond, its little head cock suddenly in recognition and look up, squinting in the sun. My heart melted. Its mother, circling on a low fly-by – 'What the hell are you doing on that boat!' Then the chick opened its beak! Oh my! A dreadful high-pitched screech I'd been blessed not to hear sooner. Time to reunite them. Off we went, fledgling into a bucket, back to the way-point and up the cliffs. I put the bucket down within ten metres of where it had been so mindlessly assaulted, its sibling along the ledge, smug and fat on double dinners. I took pictures, like a proud mum at the school gate, as the fledgling made its way back to the edge and stood looking out. I left it there, overlooking the blue sea and white beaches, my own little bird, *Isean*, in the background.

I stayed for four days before dwindling supplies forced me on. I could have lingered for weeks there, content with the birds and the fish. I had a growing sense of belonging in these wild places. Perhaps that's not so strange. We do belong in nature, amongst plants and other animals, even if we've chosen to shield ourselves away in villages, towns and cities. As babies we were happy in mud and dirt, our fat fingers in the earth, eating worms until we learned this was incorrect. A lost connection with the wilderness can breed a nervousness, a fear of being alone in the woods. I think the kid in us still loves roaming in the wild, though, and it doesn't take long to reconnect. Like many children, I used to leave the concrete and tarmac behind, passing over playgrounds in favour of climbing trees and rolling down hills. With my brother David, I'd skip across the streaming burn at the end of our lane and I'd try to join in as he took off, fast and furious, on his bike through the park. 'Your wee sister's gallus,' I proudly overheard his friend shouting once. 'She can keep up an everythin!' Behind Dumbarton there were moorlands, the glens and ancient woodlands of Lang Craigs, an accessible little bit of countryside in the town. There's always some somewhere, even in the most urban of settings. I doubt I appreciated the woody scent of fungi and rain-soaked soil back then, but that damp, heady smell is happily triggering now. I was always mad for animals, as most kids are. I didn't get the Border collie I desperately wanted, but we had chickens and geese. I sang to my favourite, Cackles, every day. I spent most of my time with my cousin Lorraine. We used to run around the local park with plastic bags on strings, pretending they were dogs. I took a while to grow up, an innocent kid, a bit eccentric maybe. It was inevitable, perhaps, that I would eventually seek out a life closer to nature. It didn't take long, once I found my adult self immersed in that lifestyle, for those memories to resurface, that joy to rekindle; to find myself comfortable, a child again, at home in the wilderness, besotted with animals, wandering without fear, dreaming alone.

This time alone was valuable. I hadn't had much by myself as an adult. Almost all of my twenties and thirties were spent in healthy long-term relationships with decent men. Seven years with Dave, an actor I met in London when I was a newly arrived nineteen-year-old; he's still an important part of my world. Then in Brighton, at thirty, I met Phil, both of us working in theatre; I admired him from the start. A lighting designer; creative and practical, funny and kind. A grown-up. It seems often that you find what you need in life, and the decade we spent together was very happy, even through my tumult of grief and loss. He was on shore while I was in the squall, sending out that steady beam, bringing me in safely. In the end we recognised that we were dear friends above all else. When you find special people you don't let them go. We broke up with love and respect, our bond intact. It was just as I reached forty. Brave, someone said at the time. I laughed at the tactlessness, but there was truth in it. We're tribal animals, aren't we, and a bit afraid of being alone. I struggled at first. There were the practical things I couldn't do, the things I'd always left to Phil. I was unused to being by myself, started dreading long weekends and holidays, all that time to occupy. I filled some of it by going out too much. The predictable result — too many existential hangovers that left me feeling needy and hopeless. Some of it I spent on the kind of heart-breaking affair that's more appropriate in your twenties. I remember the day Tom arrived. I heard the accent first, then looked up as he sailed into my life in London and moored alongside. A mess of thick dark hair and brown eyes. Enigmatic in that annoying French way. He asked to borrow my 'ose. He had a beautiful collie. My favourite dog. Like a cosmic joke or a terrible coffee advert. I must have known immediately that it wasn't going to work. He was younger, looking for different things, but we spent years in a tangle, trying to manage a friendship that was sometimes more and sometimes less. I learned about that kind of broken heart people have, the longing that defies all sense. 'It's like asking an apple tree for oranges,' a friend's mum said. I learned that it doesn't matter that you know there's no hope; you still hope. I kept hoping for oranges and beating myself for wanting them. In the end, the tangle untangled. I said goodbye to the hope and the pain, the deep feeling of loneliness that wanting him had brought me. Because that's the thing — it's not being alone that's actually lonely. It's the feeling of absence, an unfulfilled need. It's really about self-worth, I think. I found more meaningful ways to spend my time, with people who valued me and reminded me to value myself. With friends old and new. Couples can forget to nurture friendships and I had to rebuild a social life. It was an important lesson I'll never forget, to maintain independence, keep a part of life that's yours. I had to find a balance, so that time alone at home was something to appreciate. And what do they say about being lonely? Find a hobby. I found the thing that I already loved – *Isean*. Everything I needed to be happy was already waiting for me. I just had to take the first step.

I threw myself into sailing. Small as she is, I was daunted by *Isean*. I had never been solely in charge at sea. I'd sailed with Phil and, from engine to rigging issues, left him to the problem-solving he loved while I focused on the fun. I was happily single but assumed I'd meet someone in time – it was only half a joke when I said it should be a sailor. I wanted to share my love of the sea and, secretly, I probably hoped to find someone who would teach me to sail. And so I did. *Isean* taught me to sail. I found the best love story. Reciprocal too; she rewarded my efforts and boosted my confidence. The better I got at sailing, the better she liked me – going where I wanted, behaving as I expected, cooperating. With each tiny technical achievement – checking the oil, changing the filter, practising mooring – I stopped beating myself up about all the things I couldn't do. I learned that if I quit telling myself I would mess something up, then I could usually do it. I learned the simple truth of it: we humans are incredibly adaptable. With reasons to be proud, my confidence soared, and my happiness too. That was the antidote to loneliness for me – a realisation that I could do more than I knew. That there was much more to like about myself than not. By the time I'd set off with *Isean*, I was alone most of the time but didn't feel it, because I was happy to spend time with myself.

Self-love is all very well, but it's nice to mix it up with the company of other souls. And they're easier to meet at sea than you'd imagine. There are many like-minded people sailing around, and the unique characters you find in all extreme situations, living alternative lifestyles; brilliant, clever, quirky, endlessly resourceful sailors, quick to help others. You start to recognise other boats. Maybe they helped you with your lines somewhere. Was it France? Or you anchored near them. Maybe Portugal. There's a fraternity at sea, an international community of self-sufficient problem-solvers. It's rewarding to join with other sailors for chunks of time, for company, for friendship and for practical help. Chores are hard at sea – particularly on islands with rudimentary infrastructure. Everything is a mission, all tasks take time. Dinghying to shore, only to find there's a charge to use the bins and no water available. I'd often make multiple trips, spending hours in the midday heat, weighed down with food and water, gas and diesel sourced from afar. Suddenly, sailing in company, there was help; everyone jumping into one dinghy, many hands making lighter work. Sometimes a group of us would even rent a car, stock up on all the heavy stuff and – heaven forbid – act like tourists seeing a bit of the country inland.

I sailed with the Swedes, Tjoppe and Helena, from Menorca to Sardinia and split off again, found my way to the charming little tuna-fishing town of Carloforte on the island of San Pietro. Back to the rhythm of my own slow pace, that warm welcome from locals, their curiosity ignited by the arrival of a woman sailing alone. I heard the musical enthusiasm playing out before I'd even tied up: *Bravo Bravissimo! Madonna Mia! Donna del mare!* Suddenly I remembered I'd sailed to Italy. The islanders describe themselves as Sardinian first, but the people of Carloforte have origins stretching to Liguria. It felt indisputably Italian. The street pizza, the gelato and coffee. Wonderful. The style, confidence and drama, the filmic spectacle of the evening *passeggiata*. Just being in the square with an ice cream, I felt part of it. Families greeting each other; the huge fuss over an infant in a pram; couples, young and old, strolling arm in arm; men with tiny dogs; children playing – all life was there. I met some of the happiest people I've seen anywhere. An old woman, sitting in the sun, waving me over to take her picture. Mario, in his eighties, weaving in his seafront workshop, giving away his baskets (I was on three by the time I left). You could feel how elderly people are still valued, an important part of society, not hidden away and forgotten. Loneliness surely didn't exist in this place; it positively reeked of joy. No wonder Sardinia is one of the world's blue zones for longevity. It's not just the Med diet or the sunshine. There are more valuable things that keep people healthy, vital and thriving – inclusion, self-worth and happiness. *La dolce vita* indeed. I took my time in high summer, exploring the quiet and rugged south-west coast. I anchored beside the stacked rocks of Scoglio Pan di Zucchero and by the ancient city of Nora, its atmospheric pillars and temples showcased under dramatic skies, just off our bow. A ruined Roman road, cobbled from centuries-old volcanic rock, plunges straight into the sea there; the city continues beneath the waves. Pieces of their amphorae lie hidden like gems among the waving fronds of posidonia. I stared into the water, thinking of those people doing the same old stuff we do, huffing and gossiping, loving and fighting, showing off. Timing it just right to wander that cobbled road for a glimpse of a hot neighbour . . . '*Ave*!' Dreaming. Hoping.

Autumn saw us heading north to the island's busy Costa Smeralda as it was emptying of yachts. In the Golfo di Orosei, I reached Cala Goloritzé, stopping just as darkness fell. I anchored just before a big cave, its gaping entrance barely discernible, a growl rumbling within. A little bit terrifying. 'Just the waves echoing around this dark cavernous hole,' I told *Isean*, 'and certainly not Cerberus.' No three-headed hound here. Looking up, though, there was a definite Hades atmosphere to this brooding place. Above the cave, a sharp pinnacle, pointing 150 metres up to the stars: the needle rock of Monte Caroddi pricking the sky. The moon shone down on twisted formations and limestone peaks, and just in front of the cave stood a perfect arch. The following morning I floated around as small birds swooped through the natural vault. A little further north, Cat visited, along with a terrifying storm. We were anchored by the island of Tavolara when we were hit. Maybe seventy-knot gusts. I had to harness on as I crawled to the bow to let out more chain, the rain hammering so heavily Cat needed a snorkel mask just to see me. My dinghy, heavy as it was, flew above us in the air, earning its name, *Kite*. *Isean* held fast, but a large boat narrowly avoided crashing into us, searchlights flashing and the crew shouting in panic as they were swept towards shore. Another storm weathered together. In the Maddalena islands I found perfect sailing. Smooth, flat water, sheltered by numerous islands that blocked the swell but allowed the wind. We glided along, *Isean* and I, a sail to remember, the kind that happens rarely but keeps you trying for years. We passed Budelli with its rose-pink sands, and did not glimpse Mauro Morandi, the 'Italian Robinson Crusoe' who lived on the island alone, an unofficial warden for thirty years. I wouldn't have disturbed him for anything.

In fact, I was embracing isolation to a hermit-like degree myself. I'd sometimes have to seek out civilisation and other humans. In winter they were not so easy to find – no one else was sailing – but I hoped to meet locals. I sailed to Olbia, a pleasant city in the north of Sardinia, and turned to the internet. I tried Tinder, but Tinder didn't really know what to do with me. I ditched the dating site for old-school platform Couchsurfing, where people host travellers. 'I don't need a bed for the night,' I'd start. 'But how about a coffee?' It was new for me to be so open and vulnerable, effectively asking people to be my friend. I was hugely rewarded. Too often, I'm on the edges, unable to venture inland to experience a place and its people. Now I was welcomed in by locals. Almost immediately, a young cellist called Marco invited me to dinner with his friends. It was my first visit inside a Sardinian home, and I hurried through the cold night into a firelit kitchen where they were hacking great lumps of *parmigiano* and pouring local wine. The very opposite of a clique. The next day we visited his parents' place out 'on the land', a little cottage in the country. It was like stepping into a painting, full of milk urns, jelly moulds, pumpkin husks. I was driven home to *Isean* with a basket of tiny logs for my wood burner. Then I met Piermario (he loves lighthouses, I love lighthouses) and his girlfriend Debbie (she loves dogs, I love dogs), who took me to lunch at one of their favourite trattorias for *culurgiones*, a massive treat as I rarely ate out. They understood what travellers need – showers, water, a lift to the supermarket. Kindness. I met Matteo, who wasted no time in pulling me into his social circle, an exceptionally lovely bunch of surfers and sailors, musicians and artists – friendships that extended all the way to family homes in Rome. I went to dinner parties and to picnics up Monte Pino. I found where to buy the best local wine and joined the library. As in Olhão, I was putting down roots. I took new friends sailing, hosted dinners on *Isean* – *spaghetti alle vongole* (*al dente*, of course). I lingered,

thinking of staying, as I do in every place I love. It's laughable –
even as I think of it, I know I won't. I was craving time in
wild anchorages alone, for the things you miss in a group –
the shy creatures that avoid the din of human conversation,
the flash of blue and orange, a kingfisher in the stillness. I was
missing the journey.

People avoid sailing in winter, but it's my favourite time,
greedy for all those beautiful spots to myself. In February I
headed into the Bonifacio Strait, where the strong Mistral
winds funnel between Sardinia and Corsica. I made for the
Lavezzi archipelago, a scattering of little granite islands and
reefs. I arrived, spooked, at the atmospheric Île Ratino, eyeing this dramatic jagged coastline – as beautiful as it is
unsettling. Everything was dark. I'd grown used to Sardinia's
nice white sandy bottoms. Now I was weaving through sub-
merged rocks and reefs in fading light. The sea was black
(weeds, rocks or dark sand), making it hard to anchor. The
desolate anchorage entrance was marked by colossal boulders
stacked on boulders as if by giants. Strangely beautiful. Otherworldly. And unnerving. Suddenly I felt quite alone in this
lunar setting. It's easy to let a slight panic build in unfamiliar
places and begin to doubt the whole enterprise. 'Why am I
here by myself, sailing in winter?' I fretted to *Isean*. 'If it all
goes wrong, it will be entirely my fault.' Then I lit my wood
burner and sat outside acclimatising. I watched the smoke rise
from the chimney under darkening skies and a full moon rising. I listened to the whistling wind and monitored our
position against the twisted rocks. *Isean*'s saloon flickered in
candlelight, a warm cosy glow, inviting and reassuring. All is
well. We were holding. I started to relax and enjoy this strange
moonscape, embracing the very particular wonder of being at
home in such an alien setting. I was in France suddenly and
briefly, so I marked it with wine and a chicken cassoulet. I ate

by the crackling stove. Happy. I was full of the privilege of my place in the world, full of love for my little boat, always keeping me safe and comfortable. I had found the balance I needed between company and solitude. Each was important, but solitude – so hard won – was most precious of all. I hadn't set out to be alone, but after a time I found that I loved it. Then I found that I needed it.

II

A battle! Three men stood on Giglio harbour wall and watched as I fought high winds that accelerated from the land. I tacked back and forth, avoiding rocks on the approach, inching forward. Half an hour later, they were still watching. Same old, same old. People do like a show, and with this wind, I was quite likely to give them one. I reached the entrance, put my sails away, switched to the engine and prayed for an easy spot to land. Giglio, a windy little place, it turns out, is one of seven islands in the beautiful Tuscan Archipelago. It lies fifty miles east of Corsica and roughly ten off the Italian mainland. It was my second stop in Italy proper. The first had been pretty Marciana, a town that tumbles down to the sea from Monte Capanne on the island of Elba. It was late February, and the same gales that had sent me running for shelter there had closed off public buildings in Rome, claimed at least four lives and swept a cargo ship onto shore on the other side of the country. The wind was still blowing hard when we left. I rounded Giglio harbour entrance at thirty knots. A small port, a big car ferry – the *Isola del Giglio* – quite a lot to hit, and no room for error. The men were still there and, I now realised, were coastguard officers. They were shouting and gesticulating. I followed where they pointed, to a safe space behind their boat. I threw the line but missed the cleat as gusts drove me towards shallow water. The quick thinking of one of them, grabbing my stern line, brought me to a safe, if undignified, halt. They must have waited half an hour, at the end of the day, to help me. They got me tied up and left me to it. No charge, no paperwork, no intrusive questions, no 'where's the skipper?'; just an efficient and caring welcome into their port. Someone told me later that the Giglio coast-guard is a family outfit, and it certainly felt like it.

With a reception like that and an exhilarating sail, I was practically skipping when I went for a stroll past the colourful quayside houses. I must have looked a bit wild, blowing into this quiet little place just after a big storm. It was unusual enough for a boat to arrive in winter, even more so for a small boat. For a small boat with just a woman on board in winter after a storm – that was unheard of. And whether people thought I was brave or loco, they certainly noticed me. Every single person I met smiled and said hello. '*Ciao! Buonasera!*' I called back, with alarming enthusiasm. I was irrepressibly happy, on the move again. I probably looked like a slapstick character from a silent movie, all exaggerated cheerfulness, petting dogs along the way, stopping to pick up an old man's cane as he beamed at me, returning blown-off laundry to racks and spilled litter to bins. A proper little do-gooder. I should have had my own jaunty theme tune. Perhaps I was finally getting into the Italian spirit. I was experiencing some-thing special – the islands off season. In winter, the locals, not yet jaded with tourists, made time for this strange British sailor. One day I walked four miles uphill to a small fort on the top of Giglio, cars tooting and waving all the way. I rested by some allotments where an old man sat in smart clothes. He was frozen in mid-task, one hand holding an enormous white lily, the other clutching a pruning knife. I followed his gaze, past the conifers and warm terracotta roofs, to the navy-blue Tyrrhenian Sea and pastel skies. A picture-perfect scene. I carried on before he noticed my intrusion, all the way to Giglio Castello. Even up there people knew who I was – island life! The fort wasn't the highest point, so on I went, scrambling over rocks and tree trunks, hopping over pulsating balls of larvae; deranged, sweaty, exhausted, determined to get to the peak. Finally, I came to the very top of the island, where falcons and kestrels flew. I sat on the warm stones with the lizards in the evening sun, looking out to sea. Somewhere over there, Rome. Terrifically exciting. I stared at the harbour below, where I could see my little boat tied up to the wall – there she was, *Isean*! The little boat that had brought me all the way from England. Sitting up there, higher than the castle, I felt like a king. The gods must have noticed my pride with displeasure. I was in their territory now. I particularly worried about that old rogue Zeus. I'd be wandering forests, singing and collecting pine cones for the fire, or skinny-dipping in some hidden bay, and I'd imagine that serial abductor looking down, or turning up as a greedy bull or a swan, obviously attracted by my chastity and virtue, my innocent melody. Be careful! You'll end up an insect or bearing cygnets, and that would be a nightmare on *Isean*.

Alas, my insolence incurred his wrath, or maybe his brother Poseidon's, for on the next day's sail to the island of Giannutri, an earthly slip of crescent moon, I had horrible conditions and my head in the clouds. I made multiple errors, rushing to get safe ahead of high winds in fading light. Dark clouds gathered in furrowed lines above my head. I made for the half-moon island, covered in juniper and heather, in winter inhabited mainly by gulls. I hoped to use Spalmatoio's summer ferry pier and raced into the tiny bay to find – of course – that it was unusable, and the depth went from too shallow to abyssal. I tied on while I thought things through and *Isean* bounced around in objection, her low decks lining up with the underside of the rough cement landing stage. I hastily cast off, got my rope caught in the prop and lost the engine. There was no option. I stripped off. Clutching a knife, I went into the black water as the boat – all five tons of her – bounced dangerously above my stupid head. I twisted my back cutting the tightly wound rope, then leapt aboard, restarted the engine and steered through the rocks in building wind. *Isean* behaved impeccably but I was quite a sight: bad-tempered, naked and bleeding from barnacle cuts. I finally got the anchor down, praying to Poseidon it wouldn't drag through his slippery seaweed or snag under rocks so that I'd have to dive with a weak back. Then I prayed to leering old Zeus that he go easy on the winds and leave out the thunderbolts. I was no king, just a small naked thing on a tiny boat, bruised, battered and bleeding. I remembered my place. Down into *Isean*'s warm cabin I went, kettle on, storm chocolate in hand, and headed for bed. 'It's okay,' I told myself, for once not crying. 'I will be able to deal with whatever happens. Furthermore,' I added, 'in the morning everything's going to feel better and this will just be another lesson.' The gods must have decided I'd suffered enough, for we held in the tiny bay as the wind whistled around that thin sliver of land. And my recovery was swift, according to my logbook two days later. 'I am so content right now,' I raved. 'So happy. Light breeze on the beam, four knots – almost enough to make Fiumicino before dark. My back has eased up. Cuts and bruises healing and *Isean*'s engine is okay.' I'm not surprised I was happy – Fiumicino is on the outskirts of Rome.

And I was back in rhythm with the sea. A fright, particularly of your own making, shocks you out of a complacency that can creep in when you spend your every waking – and sleeping – moment on water. It's quite a useful exercise to imagine those gods frowning down too, an overview from above, a reminder of our frailty. No more slovenly departures and slipping attention; back to being respectful, noticing the detail: the water's changing light and colour; its beds of weed and grass, sand and rocks; the surface ripples, the currents and bubbles; the steady gentle swell that will build into heavy waves. I had become so used to the landscape passing, turning from mountains to fields to cliffs, the colours changing, the fluidity and constant movement of nature as we travelled through it. Everything in my life was motion. I was, therefore, quite overwhelmed by my arrival in Rome, by its structure and solidity, its devastating beauty. A place where you stumble upon crumbling columns like litter in back streets. My first visit to this eternal city. I was welcomed into the family home of Sardinian friends in the quarter of Trastevere. From there, I walked with Daria, a photographer with an eye for light. We wandered Gianicolo in the early hours, stood on the hill and watched the city spread below, blinking as the sun rose. Quite something, awakening from my watery world to all this wonder – the Vatican, the Colosseum, the Pantheon, the Altare della Patria, the Spanish Steps. I stared up at pillars and domes, across ancient piazzas, at Byzantine mosaics and Renaissance frescoes. I sat at Salvi's Trevi Fountain with a slice of pizza, reminded there is beauty that man has made. I watched happy people thronging onto streets, youngsters posing, an old couple fondly smiling at each other, and I experienced that overwhelming emotion you can get sometimes just observing humans enjoying themselves.

I felt a bit removed from it all, an alien observer, not of this world, just passing through. I was glad of it. Happy to recall how much I love about land, about culture and my fellow humans. And my time there was made by people. Back to the little boatyard in Fiumicino where everyone downs tools to gather for lunch and I was drawn into preparing the pasta. Amid the communal tomato-quartering and discussion about how much basil – *quanto basta* – we raised a chianti to sailing plans. I was excited about my return to sea. We flew south, *Isean* and I, eager to reach the stunning Amalfi Coast. I had been rehearsing a dream. I would anchor just past Positano, where the Ristorante Da Adolfo shoves up against the cliffs, a little gem in the form of a shack with a charcoal grill. I'd order the mozzarella on lemon leaves, grilled fish, a carafe of chilled wine. This was going to be my big treat. I'd been praying for the right weather, checked the charted depth; everything had lined up perfectly. But something was wrong as I headed in. No chatter, no glasses clinking. No Da Adolfa. I stared in confusion at an empty platform. It was March – the place hadn't been built yet. I rowed there and sat forlornly with a little cat who seemed as hungry as me. I sailed to Amalfi and fought hordes to buy a few overpriced vegetables. As I headed back to *Isean*, anchored in front, a local advised me that the winds would be worse than forecast. I should seek shelter, he said. With foreboding, I went into the harbour and asked the coast-guard for permission to tie to the empty wall – often, they say no. Better to do it first and plead ignorance after. Sure enough, they refused entry. Furthermore, I couldn't pay to moor on the visitor pontoons because it wasn't yet April and that was the rule. Yes, even in bad weather. Exasperated, I went back to *Isean* and lost no time sailing off into the windy, cold, dark night. Dinner cancelled. Best not tell Cat.

I arrived in Salerno near midnight, miserable, hungry and exhausted. I found a safe place to tie on a wall near the coast-guard boat. Forbidden, no doubt, but I would deal with it in the morning. Bad move. The rapping came early. Uniformed men told me to shift myself. I appealed to them, pointing to the building winds and the fact I was alone. Could I stay for the day? A superior officer turned up, small, handsome and furious. He demanded I leave: 'NOW!' It makes me laugh how we have accepted the fiction that women are the more emotional gender. It's a narrative that only works if we pretend anger isn't a feeling. I met so many emotional men, all bruised pride and sulky questioning as I had the temerity to stop them stepping on to my boat and taking charge. Why was I happier on my own? Was I 'into women'?' 'Oh, I get it, you're a weird loner.' In Salerno, it was a case of high indignation, for I was, admittedly, in the wrong. He was, therefore, well within his rights to be EXTREMELY ANNOYED. And I didn't respond well, tired, hungry and over-sensitive. We argued heatedly. He screamed, 'I AM THE COASTGUARD!' My adolescent response – 'Yes, but are you human?' – didn't help. His associates, a pair of lovely men, did help, and I was eventually given a safe place. Their kindness – helping me tie on – reduced me to tears. I spent a couple of stormy days in Salerno, an elegant city, but I didn't enjoy it. I watched a young woman skilfully manoeuvring a boat in the harbour and felt ashamed of myself for making a fuss. It occurred to me that I must have appeared strange to the authorities – why wasn't I just in a marina? The coastguard probably didn't understand what I was doing, roaming around trying to find free places to stay. I hadn't handled that situation well. Trying to put it behind me, I set off south, around the rugged Campania coast, where I found cathedral-like shelters, lovely harbours – Acciaroli and Camerota – and friendly people. I went for quiet walks and swam in refreshing spring seas. But I found no joy.

Wheesht! She's like a kid, crying in her bed. 'It's so unfair!' Yes! Life is unfair! Come on! Were you looking for sympathy?! It was your decision to be alone at sea. You didn't want special treatment. The first sign of trouble, it's all self-pity? We don't need to go where we're not allowed. I can hold anchor! We've been in much worse. Get over this nonsense, up and about, time to move on. Wheesht! I do feel for her, but I need her strong.

She's improved, I'll give her that. Learned that she must play her part in this partnership. Don't just hope our sails will outrun dark storm clouds. I can't do it all myself. She must trim those sails, to speed us, to clear that squall, or reef them to keep us safe if we are caught. I admit I'm not perfect. I never point where she wants in reverse. 'Isean!' she sighs. 'Just going off your own way!' I know, I know. Men laugh and shout from the quay. All the way from Scotland to Spain, the same old jokes. Women drivers. She shrugs it off. Those men don't know boats. Look at my long keel, sheathed and perfectly weighed. How I curve so gracefully a metre and a half through the water. It means I don't steer well backwards. It means I cut easily through heavy waves. And what's more important?

Coming in from the sea, I remind her I can help. Put on my engine, that's it, on tick-over; now I can gently circle. A nice little orbit. You drop the sails. Take all the time you need. I'll keep us from danger. Ahead of bad weather, she sends prayers to our anchor – please keep us safe in this storm, please hold Isean while I'm gone – but it's she who has set the anchor well. She has learned to look after us both, to change the oil, grease the winches, soak our lines, stiff from sea water. To undo damage caused by salt in the sea. She takes care of me. So I can better care for her. We work well together. A sistership.

I ordered a *caffè latte* at the Petit Bar in Cetraro's historic centre, deserted but for my old friend Poseidon – Neptune here – and his trident atop a nineteenth-century fountain. Suddenly, a commotion at the door. A bunch of wise guys, shouting, gesticulating, competing for attention, a frenetic energy and the strong smell of testosterone – or maybe Paco Rabanne. There was a hard eighties vibe: an old thin guy with a white ponytail and a green and pink velour jumpsuit; a small stout guy with a short mohawk in a red striped tracksuit; a guy in sharply creased trousers, shiny head and mirrored shades. And very showy. He had paid for my coffee, I was told by the weary waiter, as he brought it to the pavement table. I tried to decline, and failed – '*già fatto!*' – then kept my distance as they loudly joked and jostled, discussing me, grinning across. It was moderately funny, in a bizarre and deeply uncomfortable way. Cetraro had looked so promising from the sea, a port overlooked by an attractive old walled town on a hilltop. *Isean* and I had crossed from Campania to Calabria, Italy's poorest region, and as we approached, the difference was striking. I'd been looking forward to escaping the tourist spots – and I'd definitely done that. No more stunning Amalfi cliffs, or the green coastal towns and pleasant beaches of Cilento national park. If I wanted authenticity, I had it in spades. Here was a forlorn dirty grey beach, a mess of industrial and domestic rubbish, backed by a confusing system of dual carriageways and flyovers. I had headed up to the old town in the morning, accompanied by numerous cars slowing, tooting and gesturing out of the window. I'd had that on the islands, but this had a different feel, more men openly staring than friendly waving. I'd found that one café open on the hilltop square, where I was joined by this ridiculous mob. Then one of the guys who had kerb-crawled me on the way up drove past, hanging out of the window, making bizarre faces at me. He did it over and over, round and round the square. Time to leave. On the road I waved on the mohawked guy as he slowed and tooted. He approached me at the bottom. I should have taken his lift, he signalled. I should not walk alone. It was mid-afternoon.

The seafront, I was relieved to see, was busy with couples strolling. Normality. I wandered along to social-housing tenements on the promenade, kids playing in gardens scattered with fishing nets and small boats – a contemporary fisherman's village. A cheering family atmosphere. Nearby, I noticed a tiny guy, smartly dressed in a black shirt and white trousers, grinning as I took pictures. We had a short, stilted conversation in which I politely rebuffed him, and then he followed me everywhere, first on foot and then by car, crawling along, window down, like something out of Elena Ferrante's fifties Napoli. *Vuoi venire? Dai. Perché no? Dai vieni. Vuoi venire? Perché? Hai paura?*' ('Are you scared, come on, why not?') His wrists waggled around, oversized watch and gold bracelet hanging. Trying to coax me into the car. Sneering, he said, '*Sola, barca, marina.*' That threw me. He knew I was alone on a boat. I remembered the marina manager announcing to a restaurant the night before that I was a brave woman of the sea. Everyone in this unsettling place seemingly knew everything. I went from my initial politeness to irritation but kept it in check – this is how we stay safe. Get the balance right; don't act like a victim, don't antagonise, don't be too angry or strong. Above all, don't laugh at him. Don't tip this twisted game of cat and mouse into something worse. He's still smiling; this is still courting, Cetraro style.

I'd had plenty of hassle on the trip. Hardly surprising. I was a novelty. At first I found it strange that I attracted attention simply in sailing alone. I laughed when someone in Portugal introduced themselves by saying, 'I heard about you in Spain,' and when a harbour master gestured to the cabin, nodding, 'Do you have a man down there?' In time, though, I became more jaded – by the probing questions, by men staring, taking photographs right under my nose. Behold the *woman*, lifting her anchor! There were the pushy drunks disturbing my peace, more nuisance than threat, their mates sniggering along as I had to abandon the simple pleasure of sitting in my cockpit. Be the one guy who says, 'Leave her alone,' I always thought, as no one met my eye. Then there were dodgier times in deserted harbours at night. I preferred being anchored in the wilderness than in the supposed safety of a port. Shelter from the sea sometimes came at the cost of feeling unsafe on land – men loitering too long, looking too hard, stepping on my boat, invading my space. It was when I was no longer alone that I noticed how deeply ingrained the unease was. In a busy harbour, I'd drift off to sleep with the thought that shouldn't have to form: 'Safe here.' Neighbours to hear if something happens. The something we dread. You don't consciously think about footsteps coming in the night, but it doesn't take much to awaken that fear. Certainly, in Cetraro the harbour would not offer protection. I tried to shake off this vile man for hours, his car U-turning in persistence. At one point, I cut off the road and onto the deserted grey beachfront, only to find him juddering along the sand towards me. A nervous walk home and I didn't get much sleep that night, moving *Isean* to anchor at sea in the dark. 'Oh, Cetraro! They don't get many women there,' laughed Anna, a vivacious Italian woman I met later. 'Especially not travelling and especially not alone!' A Calabrian friend put forward a theory. 'There are a lot of sex workers there. If you were walking alone, yes, even in jeans, they probably thought you were a prostitute.' Another perspective from friends made in Sicily: 'Ahhh, Cetraro, a big Mafia area.' The Ndrangheta.

On a fast mission to get out of Cetraro, I rowed ashore at first light and went looking for gas. I'd been directed to a shop beside the social-housing block and met a man coming out of the building. No, he told me, not there. He was so kind, falling over himself to help, calling me back – I'd dropped my wallet. He flagged down a friend with a car. I was wary but sensed a decency in him and jumped in. The garage was closed – but they offered to take me back the next day. I was so touched. There is kindness everywhere, good people in the hardest circumstances – and that town must have been a hard place to live. Still, I was not touched enough to stay in Cetraro another day. Off I went, late, in a rough sea on a sixty-mile sail without gas, no hot water for coffee – sob! – and just raw vegetables to eat. Rather than risk any more run-ins with the dodgier locals, I headed off empty. By the second day, *Isean* was doing all the work while I catnapped, feeling sorry for myself under my blanket. I heard a commotion outside and came up to find rowdy dolphins breaching energetically all around us – a cacophony of clicking and splashes and fun. What an awakening! They stayed with me, bow-riding on the energy of *Isean*'s wave, flukes beating, pectoral fins steering, jostling and nudging for position. The water was so clear you could see the markings, a patch of cream curving up into light grey, the paler white underneath, the smoky eyeshadow around the eyes – eyes staring straight back at you as they turn for a good look. The best companions, always cheering you up. 'Catch up, catch up, it's springtime, what fun.' How could you not smile? They saw me a good chunk of the way down to Tropea. I sat on the bow watching them roll and whistle through the water – thank you! – until they left and I headed south to anchor outside the harbour. I was fit to drop.

Still no gas, no food and not much sleep. No sooner had I dropped anchor than a fishing boat approached with an uncouth man trying to sell me things, his constant monologue punctuated only by noisy spitting over the side. Fish, did I want fish? No? Then what? Did I want to go into the marina? Did I need to buy anything? What did I want? I wanted peace but I wasn't getting any. He was relentless. In the end, tired and weak, I let my guard down, admitting that I needed gas. I realised my error too late. He wouldn't give up until I'd given in. My judgement was off and I found myself in his boat, especially stupid since I had my own dinghy. Still, the harbour would have gas and I'd be back in five minutes. But then – oh God, no! – I was ushered onto the back of his 50cc scooter. A precarious ride up a steep hill to the town at the top, the bike spluttering, him spitting, almost mowing down children as he stroked my legs. With one hand on the back of the bike and one on my gas bottle, I couldn't slap him off, but I pushed him away as he hovered over my shoulder at the ATM, then he sold me an overpriced gas bottle from his mate. I got back to *Isean* and – what sweet reward! – coffee. I might have been ripped off and lightly molested, but it was worth it. I slept soundly that night, too tired to worry about the spitting figure outside. And I woke in the morning to find that Tropea was stunning. In different circumstances I would have stayed. A medieval cliff-top town, built by Heracles, legend says. If I hadn't been so distracted by grubby hands, I'd have seen that its main square – Piazza Ercole – was named after him. I sat in *Isean*'s cockpit and stared up at this ancient town rising out of the cliffs. Breathtaking palazzi, beautiful faded mansions in watercolours of yellow, pink and orange carved right into the rock face, a sheer cliff plunging straight down to us. The sea was clear and calm, emerald waves lapping an empty white beach. In the early morning, horses galloped along the sand; one brown and at its rear one white beast, pausing as it looked out towards us. A scene as timeless as it was beautiful. Magnificent animals. Diomedes' mad mares, I decided. Man-eating horses, captured by Heracles and driven to sea. If they were hungry, I could point them in the direction of a snack. I watched them go, lifted anchor and headed south to Sicily.

I woke up in the morning and heard the engines throbbing. The Guardia di Finanza had pulled up beside me. A militarised police force, on the lookout for financial crime and trafficking. '*Buongiorno!*' I emerged, a forced smile on my face, but they had no time for niceties and a lot of time for angry glaring. I had to move. I was on sand and doing no harm, but the bay had that day been designated a protected area. I tried for empathy. 'I have to lift anchor by hand,' I explained. 'I have a bad back. Could I have a little time, please?' More hostility, more glaring. I must go IMMEDIATELY. They circled aggressively while I sat on the bow, taking my time to lift the chain. Round and round they went, creating a wake that rocked me dangerously as I struggled with my anchor in the swell. '*Grazie*,' I called. '*Grazie mille.*' British sarcasm, entirely lost on them – just as well lest I find myself with a fine. As I sailed away, half a mile off the coast a powerful RIB speeded at me, the Guardia Costiera, part of the Italian navy – search and rescue, maritime law enforcement, military readiness. And they were in a high state of readiness, pointing and yelling at me. I must go farther out; five miles, the new rules say. I sailed off on my harmless little boat, while they crashed around with their massive engines, caring nothing, I would bet, for this newly protected zone.

With a few notable exceptions in Italy's south, run-ins with the coastguard made me less safe at sea; the approach of official boats brought severe men barking orders. I'd noticed a sharp increase in checks south of Rome, multitudes of coastguards, often armed. They'd be a welcome sight, no doubt, if you were in serious trouble, but rescue is just one of their functions. The policing role is crucial here, with illegal fishing and drug-smuggling rife, especially in the Mob-infested south. And it was hardly surprising to find a forceful border control looking for human traffickers, given the proximity of the African continent, and the thousands of people smuggled north to Italy annually. Perilous crossings in flimsy boats led to the loss of many lives at sea. Humanitarian ships patrolled these waters, searching for vessels in distress, and in an increasingly febrile political atmosphere, began to attract criticism for creating a 'pull factor'. Some were even accused of colluding with smugglers. Criminalising rescue was becoming the norm. Just as I reached the toe of the Italian boot, lawmakers, led by the country's deputy prime minister, Matteo Salvini, had proposed a 5,500-euro fine per person saved and imprisonment for those landing rescued migrants and refugees. Sicilian fishermen facing the situation we'd faced in Spain risked court and bankruptcy to help desperate people. Still, NGO volunteer crews, and Italian coastguard officers at all levels, chose to uphold the principle of rescue at sea and had to battle to do so.

As I arrived, Pia Klemp, a German who captained the rescue ship *Iuventa*, was under investigation by the authorities for 'aiding and abetting illegal immigration'. As I left, another German, Carola Rackete, was charged with 'resistance and violence against warships' after landing sick people in Lampedusa for the charity Sea Watch. Salvini called it an act of war and branded Rackete a pirate. I could well imagine the rage of the coastguards whose orders these women defied. In the south, I often felt hostility, and I wasn't heroically skippering a rescue ship, I was selfishly sailing a tiny boat for pleasure. Even so, I attracted attention. The southern Italian coastline was littered with abandoned yachts used for trafficking, so I quickly understood that a boat with a lone sailor stood out. But once I'd been checked, the suspicion only increased. It usually went from surprise to annoyance that there was no real skipper – a man – to speak to. Casual misogyny, I figured, but with a twist, it turned out. I was later told it was just so unusual for a woman to sail by herself I would have looked like a real trafficker. I couldn't be out there for pleasure.

It must be work – drug-dealing or trafficking. What was I doing at sea alone?

Women at sea have always been met with suspicion. In the recent past, there were only two places we were meant to be – bare-breasted on the figurehead of a ship, or on the quay, awaiting the return of our men. At the very least, we were considered an unlucky presence on a boat, but in ancient myths, women at sea are worse than unlucky, they're down-right dangerous – the Sirens, half birds, half women, bewitching passing sailors with their song; Circe on Aeaea, the sorceress and daughter of the sun, turning Odysseus's men into swine. And then there's Scylla, my own favourite, the multi-headed sea monster who regularly devoured sailors with each of her grotesque mouths. I was now right on her doorstep – at the Strait of Messina. Gruesome, Homer said. Deathless evil. No sailors ever passed her unharmed. But Homer didn't know women could sail. Men feared her but I wouldn't – she'd be a sister to *Isean* and me. I nosed into the harbour of her namesake town, Scilla, right at the entrance to the strait. It's a beautiful place, divided by a promontory with a castle – Castello Ruffo di Scilla – and a lighthouse that beams down on the rocky strait. To the south-west, a sweep-ing beach and a town that rises up to a mix of old and new. And wandering down and round to the east of the castle, the little quay and charming old district of Chianalea, with nar-row alleys and old fishing houses right on the water's edge. That's where we were heading, for it offers protection from the fierce winds that blow through the strait. And we were, as usual, seeking shelter from a storm. There were just a few open fishing boats tied up, even smaller than *Isean*. It didn't look like a place for visitors. I motored around, frowning at the seabed – I didn't fancy anchoring amid rocks in a gale. I saw fishermen returning to harbour on a small boat.

'*Buonasera*!' I smiled in hope, determined to stay open, to keep trusting my instinct and not let those few miserable men jade me.

I was right to. It's always right to. As I did everywhere, I found wonderful kind men in this region. Men like Marco Miuccio, a coastguard on nearby Salina island. A novelist, poet, and finalist in Italian *Masterchef*, he made me laugh, all six foot of him, in brass-buttoned uniform, walking his tiny black poodle. He looked down at me and *Isean* as we begged for storm shelter in Salina harbour. 'You came all the way from England? In this?' A thumbs-up. 'In you come.' Take too the fishermen of Stromboli, the Cusolito brothers. Big, bearded bears of men, salty lined faces mobbed with curls, bulging dad forearms and beefy hands hacking huge chunks of fish. They personify rugged masculinity . . . then they open their mouths. The tenderness in their words, speaking of the sea, reciting poetry to the volcano – it could move you to tears. Full of gentleness, fathoms of feeling. Men make up half of all my favourite people on Earth. And both my sailing heroes. You can't get much more heroic than the first man to sail single-handed around the world. Step forward Nova Scotian Mr Joshua Slocum, who did it at the end of the nineteenth century. A delightful mix of Victorian masculinity and emotional fluency, revelling in the sea's poetry and singing to porpoises. The enigmatic French sailor Bernard Moitessier was all feeling on his circumnavigations, looking for love from shearwaters flying overhead. He spoke of his boat with a touching sentimentality I recognise. *Joshua* (named after Slocum), he wrote, was so happy one time he feared 'she might try something new'. Our boats. We know them.

I was struck by these men, sailing fifty and a hundred years ago: how closely their feelings matched my own. Perhaps it was simply in their being at sea – the romantic sea – far from the pressures of society and free of the expectations placed upon men that allowed such tenderness. Reading their words was like holding up a mirror. I feel feminine but, especially at sea, draw on qualities that we have somehow decided are masculine. I believe my most feminine quality is my strength. When I've been tested, I feel my mother's strength in my core. I think she left it to me. It's not always there, but it comes when I need it. When things are going to get rough, I sense it, a stoicism that feels innately female. A time to be solid and strong, to be calm and hold on. To protect and dig in. To get through. It's about survival. That's the most feminine thing I can think of. But this thing, this force, I recognise as feminine, I don't see it only in women. I've seen this strength in men too, drawn from gentleness and empathy. It's harder for men to show. Women are encouraged to follow the heart. To feel things, not to repress. My father, like the Stromboli fishermen, is a mix. A poet, full of emotional courage, and a grafter who learned from his shipbuilding father to be tough. His instinct to be strong for his family is so great that his pain seems, he says, a weakness I shouldn't witness. Crying is an impossible feat, a physical struggle. It's harmful, I fear, to hold pain in, for it comes out somehow, in stress, anger or violence, anxiety or illness. We've done a lot of damage with those rigid gender roles, the burden of what we're supposed to do and be. Hopefully, that's beginning to change as younger people take a more fluid approach to life. Out at sea, where you draw on all your reserves – masculine and feminine – to get through, it's fluid too. There's only one role really, and it's human.

Back in Scilla, my enduring trust in the decency of men was paying off. A broad smile from Damiano the fisherman, who was exceptionally considerate. '*Si, si*,' he said, pointing to the wall. There was room, it was deep enough. I tied up, next to a bunch of locals fishing. I was so glad to be in and safe – to have gas for hot water – that I effusively made espressos for all the men there. I heard them reassure each other that it was okay, I had a moka pot, the coffee was Italian. I finally felt happy. Later, though, the harbour felt different. It was out of the way and by night was deserted. I was awakened at 3 a.m. by a steady stream raining above my head – some guy pissing down on *Isean*'s deck. Then, I heard the rest of them, along the quay, a load of men shouting, kicking, smashing things. They started singing in a loud chant, maybe football, maybe not. I felt my heart race as I hurriedly dressed and watched out of my window, wondering if they knew I was alone. I was ready to run. I was there to shelter from a storm, but the only thing that stopped me from leaving was the knowledge that I might reveal myself before I'd got *Isean* off the wall. Eventually they left – my fears unwarranted. But I was on edge. I'd felt hunted the whole way down the southern coast. My bigger fears hadn't been storms or boat problems or ships or other dangers at sea. Jokes of predatory gods had materialised in mortal form. I'd watched that mindless gang, that pumped-up pack of men, with my heart beating, eyes wide, adrenaline kicking in – pure instinct, like a gazelle ready to run into a storm. Better gale-force winds and high waves than being pissed on by a drunken mob. I don't like to think of myself cowering there in the dark, though. Or running like prey, all the way down that coast. It doesn't suit me. I spent most of my time at sea dreaming, so I will allow myself a heroic retelling of this voyage.

No, I did not run. I channelled the wit and sorcery of Circe, the draw of the Sirens, the bravery of Klemp and Rackete. 'Come,' I said to that tiny predator in Cetraro, 'a drink on board, and forget home and family.' The sly smile spread across his face, but soon it waned. So small and malleable once the potion kicked in, he was easily lifted. I placed on his head a wreath of thistles. Sea-purple. A symbol of my homeland, picked on Calabrian shores. I affixed him, this feeble figurehead, on Isean's prow, and her sails spread wide on either side, snowy white, the wings of a goose. My turn to smile. I rose and the wind filled my hair like a sail, whipped and salty, wild with curls. Like Helios on his chariot we ascended, but I carried no whip, for Isean needed no direction. We were two sides of the same thing. Soaring, half me, half her. We flew over the Costa degli Dei — this coast of the gods — past rumbling Stromboli, its fire raging into the sky; past the fishermen reciting poetry; my father proud to see me fly. We passed Aeolus' floating island; a hospitable king, he sent us the Zephyr. West winds. Arabian horses. Mares galloping; one port, one starboard; one silver, one chestnut brown; aqua eyes, deep pools shimmering, manes flowing, tails high and proud.

We were fast carried south to Heracles' own port. There they left, one look back, they wished us well. We coursed through azure seas, and yet we were not alone. Racing dolphins took up our journey, streaking like lightning, whistling in friendship, gliding gracefully before the bow — we had the protection of friends, and the guards of this coast would give us no trouble. We reached the lair of mighty Scylla herself. Isean pushed forward to the cavernous mouth. She would do what was required. The waves licked up around the feet of our passenger, rousing him from the powerful effects of his drink. I watched his confusion, recognised the feeling in those first moments of waking. Where am I? Am I safe? No. No, you're not. He had woken with foreboding already upon him. I felt a flicker of empathy, for the boy he had once been, but I would not spare the man he had become. Too late, he realised his mistake. He had thought himself a hunter, but he was a coward, afraid of the sea. And his fate was still worse. It beckoned. Tentacles slithered in the darkness, a rumbling sound and then *heads — more than one — craned out, each more furious than the last. The moonlight found her, and it was impossible not to stare. All those hungry mouths gaping, roaring and writhing, and in the middle, her face, still like ivory, delicate and divine. Her hair, flowing green with stipes and fronds and blades. A terrible, beautiful sight. But we were not afraid. She looked upon us, with surprise, then with accord. Isean lurched forward, her knots untied, releasing this man, small in body and in mind, into Scylla's grip. And I was now brave enough to speak. The last thing he heard, this man who thought himself made, were my words: 'A gift, Scylla, from Isean and I.'*

12.

A rumble closer than thunder, a blow from a hole, venting, like a giant whale exhaling. A belch of fire and smoke. Iddu, they call him. For it is a he, the islanders say. I'm inclined to agree. Stromboli is alive, present, primordial. That's the earth breathing up there. *Isean* and I sailed up and down the vast empty north-western face of this volcano – Sciara del Fuoco, the huge collapse scar. It looks sheer from this angle, dark and smooth here, ridged there. Almost 3,000 metres from the seabed, rushing up in front of you; incandescent lava fragments running down the mountainside. It has been active for thousands of years, the lighthouse of the Mediterranean. Imposing, mesmerising, unforgettable. I stared and stared; nothing else existed. Time was marked only by the eruptions – every fifteen minutes, a hypnotic clock face. Five hours passed. My eye followed the smoke spiralling up, the tephra tumbling down to where earth meets sea, a mini-avalanche of molten rocks exploding into the darkness of the water. It was the sound – *pyew, pyew* – that alerted me after hours quietly watching. I noticed the jets of froth, fountains of water shooting, violent, bright white against the dark foot of the volcano. The longer I stayed, the more I saw, until after dark, when other boats came for the full roaring spectacle of fire, saffron flames licking the black sky. An extraordinary sight, but the time there alone had been truly special. Me and my boat. Infinitesimally small before all of that. As the sky darkened, I kept an eye on our position – I didn't want to drift into the path of lava. I stayed well outside the markers, a couple of plastic buoys denoting the restricted zone. Little human notions of safety in the face of all that power. It didn't seem far enough, and a couple of months later, it wasn't. Without warning, in July and August Stromboli had violent paroxysmal eruptions that sent ash columns towering 4,000 metres into the air and pyroclastic flows advancing a terrifying kilometre across the sea – 500 metres beyond that zone. I watched videos of boats fleeing. A monstrous grey mushroom cloud, toxic fungus rushing down and billowing out over the water, expanding and rapidly rolling. The place where I had sailed in a waking dream was now engulfed in nightmarish horror; a raging inferno of hot ash careering towards a boat of screaming passengers speeding away on full throttle.

I knew that *Isean*'s little engine would never have got us out in time. Unthinkable. Stromboli's eponymous activity is explosive enough in its moderate state. In a place like that, you are reminded, several times an hour, of the fleeting nature of our silly lives, that we only just got here. We might be living in the Anthropocene, our short-sighted meddling altering the chemistry of our world, but we are no more its centre than ants on our kitchen worktop. I often felt insignificant in the vastness of the sea, but here? In the darkness, at the foot of this fire, we were nothing at all. I left in a kind of trance, heading north then east of the volcano face, looking for something like shelter. There is none. Stromboli is not an easy place to sail. Nothing about it is easy. If you asked a kid to draw a volcano, they would draw Stromboli, with its conical cartoon volcano shape and fire coming out of the top. That shape pushes winds down its steep sides, so a forecast twenty knots can be nearer forty. By dawn, the gusts were sweeping clouds of black volcanic ash over us. I shifted, anchored, shifted again. I'd planned to hike the volcano but was too unnerved to leave *Isean* alone in this extreme and brooding place. No wonder they placed Aeolus, keeper of the winds, here. It's easy to imagine some omnipotent being fanning tempests around as you bob on waves like a model boat in a bathtub. Off we sailed, half in regret, half in relief, looking back over my shoulder at the puffs of smoke regularly rising from that grand old man's pipe. I returned to the enigmatic Isola di Vulcano ahead of a storm. I knew this sulphurous little island by now, its lunar landscape and long ridges that glowed metallic orange in the sunset, its Valle dei Mostri – a mob of monsters sculpted by lava cooling on the islet of Vulcanello. I'd hiked around the smouldering crater, skirting scalding plumes of steam that shot from vents and geysers. I'd gaped into its grey and yellow cavity. In the bay below, I'd swum over the springs bubbling around our anchor and felt the cloying thermal mud ooze through my fingers. And I'd got used to the pervading and unsubtle scent of egg, an appropriate side to my easter lunch. Sailing the Calabrian volcanic arc, this active chain of islands and seamounts, all steaming fumaroles and hydrothermal vents, black sands and obsidian, was a multi-sensory experience unlike any other.

There was more wind on the way. I knew the bay would not offer much shelter from that, but it had good holding and would protect us from swell – more important, experience had taught me. I'd decided to stay on anchor, and I held my nerve as other boats ran for marinas. It's fine in theory but nerve-wracking in practice, staring at big stormy seas knowing that if your anchor drags, you're heading helplessly out into the maelstrom. I put out sixty metres of chain. I got food in – of the type that's easy to cook when you're sideways. It blew fifty-five knots, for two days. Then thunder and lightning, a gift from Zeus, as if this place needed more atmosphere. I got one hour of sleep on the first night. On day two I went out to the cockpit, leaned into a deafening wind for two minutes, then returned gasping to the uncanny quiet down below, the happy security of *Isean*'s warm saloon. How can it be, just a plank of wood separating you from that elemental fury, and down there, such peace, crackers and cheese, coffee and podcasts? Our anchor held throughout, dug deep in that thick black volcanic sand. I sent several prayers to it and threw some Merlot overboard as thanks to Poseidon for good measure (just a capful – the rest was medicinal).

After the storm, I sailed in the sweetest flotilla. Velellas. Thousands of tiny 'by-the-wind sailors': beautiful deep blue and purple hydrozoa, like baby Portuguese men-of-war. I scooped one up and was immediately charmed, a little psychedelic surfboard, tentacles underneath for eating on the go – what a life! A blue float with a transparent fin sail set at forty-five degrees. Endearingly, they have different rigs that determine direction of travel – some have sails that run north-west to south-east and they travel on a starboard tack. The others are reversed, tacking to port. *Isean* and I sailed with them for miles, tiny kindred spirits drifting around on the world's ocean currents.

It wasn't just these little sailors I felt an odd affinity with, though. It was all life at sea. Before I set sail, I'd imagined myself fit and athletic, living off fish and hunting octopus. The reality was a world apart. I stood in a foot of water as clever cuttlefish moved warily around me, changing colours and patterns. They had no reason to worry. After days spent with only curious fish for company, I had lost my appetite for fishing, preferring to watch the little sea bream that looked up to where I sat in my cockpit – if you watch, you'll see; they do look back at you. Grouper, peering out from deep rocks, 'Please don't spear me.' Swimming, I'd see different characters in the shoals over my head, some fish that seemed brave, others more shy. And why would this not be so? Ahead of a storm, anxiously looking for shelter, I'd be touched to see other creatures presumably doing the same as me: turtles heading to deeper water, all of us seeking safety somewhere. Sometimes, in bad weather, when dolphins surfaced beside me, I felt they sensed my tension, wished me well. As anthropomorphic as it is sentimental, no doubt; but why should we have the monopoly on feelings? Spend enough time alone with other creatures and that old hierarchy, the one with humans at the top, feels irrelevant. Inappropriate. Arrogant. We're so maladapted in nature, struggling to keep ourselves safe. But it's possible, I think, to regain lost ground. I began to feel a change in myself, a better connection to the wilderness. The longer I was at sea, the more I tapped into some inner knowledge. I wouldn't go so far as to call it wisdom, but it does feel like intuition, something old. I noticed, more and more, that I would have an instinct about something: which direction to go, or whether to go at all, or to avoid that patch of water – something imperceptible about it. Then I'd check and discover hazards. An unforecast storm hit on the journey I didn't take. An uncharted reef lurked. Some part of me had surely registered a subtle movement on the surface of the water, felt something in the air, as other animals do when a storm is coming. I had learned to trust my gut. In sailing, then in all things. And, in those seas in the south, I had returned to joy. I hadn't seen much wildlife in the Mediterranean, but I was spoiled in this area, thanks, no doubt, to the proximity of the Strait of Messina, one of those special places where seas meet and wildlife migrates. I was joined by a family of dolphins, their adorable calf at the bow, the smallest bundle of fun I've ever seen. Life in the atmospheric Aeolian Islands had been good, but even better lay ahead – the strait, with all the navigational excitement that encompassed, and beyond that, Greece.

The morning of my passage found me up early with that happy sense of purpose – a welcome return of the geeky sailor within. I hadn't had to think about tides since the Strait of Gibraltar a year earlier. I missed tides! I had a nice strong coffee and a focused mind as I sat on the bow lifting anchor. The wind would be building to a force six by the afternoon, but was lighter in the morning and the currents would be with us. There were counter-currents, upwellings and whirlpools to look out for. There would be dodgem fun: numerous ships and ferries to avoid, including, weirdly, one that carries the Rome–Palermo train over the sea to Sicily. Intriguing hazards. I no sooner wanted to collide with a train at sea than to hit a whale or sail into lava. I radioed the authorities on VTS Messina to tell them, with a sense of great importance, that *Isean* was in transit and about to enter the strait. What size? Ah, 8 metres, I smiled in return. 'You can proceed, lady,' the guy said, barely suppressing a chuckle. Brilliant. I was on the Sicilian side this time, looking over with some fondness at the little town of Scilla as we embarked on our best fantasy ride yet. I passed Castello Ruffo and kept a lookout for castles in the air too – the 'Fata Morgana' occasionally witnessed off the Sicilian coast. I scanned the rocks for the mouth to Scylla's lair. Nothing doing. I nodded in respect at the general area, trusting one of her sisterly heads to keep an eye on us. 'Keep us safe from Charybdis's terrible indigestion,' I whispered; 'no whirlpools today, thank you.'

The wind was light, then it pushed us sideways in a mad gust and died away again. The sea was calm but for a patch of water just ahead. Small, but what I'll call 'jacuzzi-lively', overfalls for about 500 metres. Once we were in, I could see flat water ahead, so we just enjoyed the ride. On the other side of that, two whirlpools off to our starboard. Really gentle, quite beautiful, but definitely circular pools of rotating water. Not the powerful belch I'd feared from Charybdis so much as a polite postprandial burp. I stared, mesmerised; I was having an absolute ball. In the wrong conditions this splendid confusion of intense crosscurrents, vortexes and strong upwellings is dangerous, but the main risk was in hypnotising me as we sped past on fast currents, my phone stuck on camera rather than chart.

We headed on a thrillingly fast downwind passage – reefed we made over seven knots. As we rounded Punta di Pellaro, I looked back and saw gods carved, a Doric frieze in the headland below the lighthouse. Effigies of the deities, watching in relief over our passage into Greek waters. I stared back as long as they remained in sight, overwhelmed by the beauty and symbolism on a journey that felt so ancient. We were in the wake of Odysseus. It was probably Zeus, Poseidon, maybe Hermes, god of travellers, carved there. Or perhaps it was the best of mortal men, Odysseus himself. That most human of heroes, flawed as he was. I thought of his journey as I edged my way round to the Ionian Sea. Ten years it took him to return from Troy. Quite a slog, made all the harder, I'd venture, for putting out the eye of Polyphemus, Poseidon's Cyclops son. 'Say that Odysseus, sacker of cities, blinded you,' he boasted, sailing under a barrage of rocks. Unwise for a sailor to anger the god of the sea, you might think. I'd have kept my powder dry and got home faster with a lot less fuss. A lot less glory too. I'd take the anticlimax of a safe passage over heroic tales winging their way home. Like most women, I suspect. Hopefully, there was at least one woman on display up among the gods – maybe grey-eyed Athena or pissed-off Hera. I prefer those women deemed monsters; I'd put the mighty and misunderstood Medusa up there. I reached the sole of the Italian foot and spent hours scanning charts and maps to pinpoint the exact location of this stunning statuary. I found it. There was nothing but an ordinary old viaduct below the light-house. I couldn't believe it. Even now I can see those marble sculptures carved into the cliff. They're not there. I had seen the heads of gods, but it was my own Fata Morgana on the way to Greece.

Haud yer wheesht! What's this now?! She could outsail Odysseus? The greatest hero that ever lived! He's only running after her! The cheek of it!

She laughs at his pride, and thinks she'd do better?! We're barely through the Strait of Messina! Monsters and whirlpools, Scylla and Charybdis. She's tempting the Fates, on some hero's journey!

And look at her, the would-be hero. Staring at her iPhone! Chart apps and wind forecasts, compass and GPS. And me! I'm a proper boat. I'm the reason she's at home at sea. I'd like to see how she'd have fared back then. Steering to the Bear! Skippering that galley. Squat and low to the sea. Decks wet and groaning with weight. No back-up engine, my lass. Mistrustful men on oars. A rowdy mob to control! Fighting the waves. Fighting each other. Pillaging and plundering. Swearing and shouting. Her with her 'quiet stoicism' her 'core strength'. Wheesht! Don't make me laugh!

They all want to be the hero of their own story. When will she learn? Pride comes before a fall. How quickly she forgets. All her near misses. Everyone makes mistakes at sea. Yes, even Odysseus. Too big for your boots. Talking this way! She'll anger the gods. On our way to Greece, of all places. Gods give and gods take. They'll take the wind right out of my sails.

I'd been to Greece twenty years before, with Phil. We had been staggering towards the end of winter, those horrible months after Christmas when the nights dominate and the weather is bleak. I was absorbing the reality of my mum's cancer diagnosis. Phil looked out at the blustery rain and howling wind. He looked at me, sad and sinking in the grey. Like my mum in the rain staring up at my dad on the roof all those years ago, he decided I needed some light. Sunshine and energy to take to Scotland. How right he was. How welcome it was. We arrived from a stony-cold Gatwick to colour, Cephalonia at its best approaching spring. All that lush greenery gleaming from winter rainfall, Melissani Cave and its emerald lake, the dazzling arc of white that is Myrtos Beach. I had my holiday reading – *Captain Corelli's Mandolin* – and we stayed near Sami and swam and roamed and ate well. I made regular phone calls home, long enough to hear that things were okay, to stop worrying for the day. Up in those verdant hillsides, as the bees buzzed under a warm Ionian sun, we looked to little Ithaca nestling over the mini-strait, to that place where journeys end. We didn't go there, just stared across on those days when my mum would be starting her treatment.

Maybe that's where I started my own journey, the inevitable road to a future where we would lose her. I hadn't accepted that yet, couldn't bear it. But I suppose I was setting myself in that direction. Beginning to face it, with hope as well as fear, with loving support and thoughts raised high. Of good times still to come, spring and summer, my mum's optimism and courage. Above all, I hoped for time. That the road would be a long one. It wasn't long enough. Is it ever? In the years after my mum died, I thought I was doing well. I didn't fall into a hole, but there was strangeness in my thinking. I'd joke to Phil about how I would rather lose everyone I loved right away than face their loss later. 'I should just shoot you all now,' I'd huff. 'Bam!' Must have been nice for him. I got over that, but even now, I have some twisted logic in measuring loss. Counting my blessings for pains I won't know. Like finding a strange comfort in the fact that I'll never know what it's like to lose a partner I've loved as long and as fully as my parents did. That hurt bewilderment you see in old people, alone after fifty years together. How sad to fear loving too much, too long. It goes against everything I believe about love, about being open and brave. Bereavement is hard, though. You find positives where you can. That you were on good terms. That you got to say goodbye – something so many are denied. That you were lucky enough to know that person in the first place. That's the biggest gift. We're a positive bunch, humans. Often wildly, unrealistically optimistic, finding the odds forever in our favour despite evidence to the contrary. It gets us into trouble. But the hope keeps us going.

My mum was always for hope, for moving forward. Faced with the worst news, she opted for a sense of control over feeling helpless, for happiness amid the gloom. Never, ever was she hopeless. The thing about this approach is, what's the worst-case scenario? That it was wrong to hope? That you lived your last years being positive? We think about hope often these days: whether there's much point in it, because we are living on a planet with a bad diagnosis. We all feel despair and fear. But hope has to be in the mix too, doesn't it? That's our thing. The thing that kills you in the end, some say. I felt this way about it once. When I was deep in grief and scared to be happy. I'm glad that phase passed, but I'm glad to have known it, for I cherish my hope all the more. I know it's the better way to live. It seems to be in our tradition particularly to look for positives in the bleakest times, remembering that it could be worse, that other people have it harder.

In the shock of Stephen's loss, I often felt gratitude for the terrible things it wasn't. It sounds cold, but it's human, I think, that involuntary shudder upon hearing awful news, of being glad it wasn't yours. That it wasn't suicide. Someone missing. Something unexplained, your brain trying to solve it forever. That it was not murder. It makes me think of the very worst thing I can imagine. To have been the cause of someone else's loss. To live with yourself, in the night, wake up with yourself every day. To have perpetrated evil. That must be true darkness. Socrates said it was better to suffer injustice than inflict it. We damage our souls by hurting others. We know the truth of that. You don't have to believe in karma to recognise the disquiet inside when you've done something wrong. I considered the pain and torture, the complicated anger and guilt, of the various terrible ways we lose each other, and I was thankful for the 'nice normal grief' I was left with. But that's a fiction too. For just as there's no such thing as normal, there is no such thing as normal grief. Its impact isn't something you can measure. We're all different in our responses. And each loss is different. The bad news is that going through one big loss doesn't prepare you for another. Nor should it. That wouldn't honour the people we love. Each of us is loved uniquely, each loss devastating in a different way. This is how it must be.

I burrowed in after I lost my mum, took refuge in my home. It was a quiet time. I was happy to have dodged the vertiginous grief of Stephen's death. I was naive. It was just a different process. I was stitched tightly, not to fall apart, but I hadn't escaped. How can you? Once again, in a different way, I felt a big loss of confidence. I turned inwards gradually. We're not one person all the way through life, and I became a strangely introverted version of myself. I'd just got my job at the *Guardian* and I remember those first years of work, head down, avoiding social things. I didn't turn to alcohol this time, but I must have been overeating, for I put on weight. Fine if it suits you, but my body wasn't meant for it and I was a stranger to myself. I wouldn't buy clothes because I felt good in them or because they suited me; I'd buy outfits for events purely because they would show that I had made an effort. Bizarre. In my early thirties, I felt older than middle-aged. Past everything. I'd lost myself, and I didn't even notice. A really strange thing happened. I didn't want to make new friends, I decided, because I didn't have the energy to tell them my stories. I thought I'd rather just keep the ones I had. But I wasn't seeing them either. I had forgotten how we thrive on human connections. That meeting new people, with their different energies and ideas, leads to wanting yet more friends, in the happy way that we find more energy when we do more.

It's so strange now, thinking of that person I was. I want to hug her, tell her that it's okay to trust in life, to open up again, because there will be joy and good people all around. My friends are so important now they're family. Old and new, strong and enduring, such a big part of my world. As any single person knows, they are the people who care about the details of your day and direction of your life, whose achievements mean as much as your own. Someone described an ideal romantic relationship once. It was, they said, when you're proud to be with someone. It applies to friendships too. Whenever I'm in their company, when I introduce my friends, I'm proud. Whether it's for the warmth of their characters or their intelligence and talents, their humour and empathy. For their sense of fun and adventure. I feel ridiculously grateful to have the friends I do. I consider myself lucky that they like me too. Thank God I had the good sense to find them.

And one of my very dearest found me on my birthday. *Isean* and I were anchored in Crotone, a little Calabrian town on the ball of Italy's foot. Phil came to help us across the Ionian Sea to Greece. This man carried me through some of my darkest times, and he brought *Isean* back to life from a shell in a boatyard. It was fitting that we returned to Greece together. Who better to steer my little ship while I slept? As we prepared to set off, the calm water exploded. A swordfish burst through, as from a lake to another world. Straight as an arrow, cut steel, shimmering silver, its long bill shooting up just inches away. Pure muscle. It was suspended in a moment of stillness, glistening in mid-air like a mythological beast. I took it as a good omen because I take everything as a good omen. We sailed into the night and landed in Mathraki, a small island just west of Corfu. We cruised the few miles north-east, around the top, and then zigzagged back and forth a couple of miles between mainland Albania and the Greek island. An inordinately pleasing experience to tack between countries. Phil left me in elegant old Corfu town, then on I went, down this glittering coast, to Paxos, where the water shifts in multiple shades of blue and boats bob on their own shadows.

In Antipaxos, *Isean* floated on turquoise and teal, seas so beautiful that by morning they had attracted hordes of buzzing speedboats, darting this way and that, like wasps round your breakfast. I left them and sought space at sea. It felt wonderful, drifting aimlessly away from the chaos. I made pancakes and mulled over where to go. I had no plan. That's it, I decided. Don't make one. Why not set the sails for a nice relaxing broad reach, go where the wind blows us? It blew us to mainland Greece, to Aphrodite's Cave, just north of where the Acheron flows into the sea. This river encircled the underworld, the ancients thought. Now it encircled us, tucked behind its bank to shelter from a southerly gale. Where it meets the Ionian Sea, the Acheron is unremarkable, a little murky, a narrow entrance you could easily miss. Upstream is another story. There it is clear and cold and entirely breathtaking. I swam it, through a great gorge, between high-walled cliffs; the Gates of Hades, they call it still. The barrier between the living and the dead. I was surrounded by life – fish and frogs, butterflies and electric-blue dragonflies. Birds of prey hovering overhead. It was sparkling and effervescent, fed by mountain springs. I clambered ridges and water-worn rocks, plunged gurgling pools. Elsewhere, it carried me gently, the river, flowing soft as silk. But you must be careful: the river can hurt you. With nightfall and the bats came hunting animals, and rocks tumbling down its steep cliff-side. And the river must rise and rush furiously, for I saw whole tree trunks suspended in the air, colossus boulders wedged as if Heracles placed them just so. Land of the Dead. A fine home for the night.

From there, we sailed south to the Ambracian Gulf, an inner sea that most sailors pass by; it runs greener than the crystal-clear Ionian waters they want. I'd heard it was beautiful. And so it was. In here was another world, fed by the sea and freshwater rivers, surrounded by densely wooded mountains, lakes and deltas. I ventured in and thought I might stay forever. More wildlife than I'd seen in the whole Mediterranean, and no noisy humans on speedboats. Very few boats at all. Pelicans and flamingos flew overhead; piglets trotted past clearings in the bushes; scores of turtles passed me by. Bottlenose dolphins gently rolled off my bow. By night, they hunted, tail-slapping the sea with their flukes in the dark. By day, I swam over a seabed carpeted with shifting shells, mussels snapping shut at my passing shadow, sea snails tumbling, hermit crabs scuttling. From the sand, two stingrays, like giant kites rising, whip tails like ribbons trailing behind. Then, in their hundreds, the medusas – aurelia, moon jellyfish, saucers flying by. Weightless, I glided, dodging passing planets. Off a jetty in a quiet bay, I floated above a baby cuttlefish feeding on a shell, colours changing in camouflage. Gradually, my eye was drawn to a fragile silhouette right beside me. Something I'd always wanted to see. *Hippocampus hippocampus*. Beautiful, brown; at almost ten centimetres, bigger than I knew. Then another, and one more. Three sea horses. Tails anchored to the ropes. Swaying gently, delicate snouts pointing down. At sunrise I saw their morning greeting. One to the other, they swam together, tails entwined, gently pirouetting and parting ways again. I stayed there, hypnotised at this most romantic of rituals.

I was thinking about family as I sailed this hidden world. My dad had lost two of his sisters, Violet and Margaret, and was really suffering. I needed to lift his spirits. I thought to fly him to Cephalonia, sail him to Ithaca, just to the south. I thought about my mum. I usually felt her around when I was most connected to nature, surrounded by beauty. I anchored in a bay where goats noisily hooved and bleated their way down to the sea for a salty drink at sunset. Their bells tinkled, melodic copper ringing long after their departure as they made their way back inland: 'Here we are; there we go.' I went to sleep, a juvenile cormorant perched a few metres from my pillow, all watchful in oily black. It is said that cormorants are symbols of ill omen, but not to me. I love them. They circle me when I swim near my dad's in Dunoon, getting ever closer with each revolution, yellow beaks forward, wings beating louder in my ear. Perhaps they think I'm a threat or that I have fish beneath me, for the guillemots do the same, their winter-white faces and comedy red feet. On *Isean*, I woke to a quiet dawn, all the animals still dreaming. I'd forgotten my companion and was confused as I looked out to a headless ball of fur and tail, all browns and whites, a half bird. What kind of magical creature was this? The cormorant was asleep, its long neck softly coiled, head tucked into those sleek feathers, fluffy down on display. Special, somehow, that it stayed like a sentry by my side all night. I was exceptionally happy in that peaceful gulf. Perhaps the waters of the other world found their way in there, from the Acheron flowing softly nearby. It was called the River of Woe, but in the *Suda*, it is described as a place of healing. I felt myself held there, suspended in a gentle balance. If I was on the edge of the underworld, I was perfectly at peace with it.

13

The best laid schemes o' mice an' men
Gang aft a-gley.

Robert Burns

It's a strange life sometimes. A world made of chaos. All chance encounters. Gentle nudges and violent collisions sending us this way or that. I left the gulf, sailed back out to the Ionian Sea, and south, through the Lefkas Canal. And there were the islands spread out in front of me. The mountainous peaks and dark wooded slopes of Cephalonia. Atokos, where wild pigs swim in crystal waters. Kalamos, its ghost village lying empty after earthquakes sent people running. In Skorpios, where Jackie Kennedy became Onassis, a security guy turfed us out of the picture at sunset. No accounting for taste! I made for the tiny island of Thilia as darkness fell and was driven out by swarms of angry wasps. This was the harder place to leave – a gaspingly pretty little circular bay with a single cypress tree, flashes of colour in the air – a kingfisher hunting. As the light faded, I sailed around in search of a place to rest, gaping, half in wonder, half in resentment. All those dramatic cliffs plunging precipitously into the sea. Spectacular but unhelpful for lifting anchor by hand. It's a place of great depths, and I exhausted myself repeatedly hauling metres of chain as my anchor stubbornly refused to set. Eventually, I ventured into the quiet haven of Abeliki Bay in Meganisi island. And there the unthinkable happened. The start of the season, 1 July. A chartered flotilla arrived, inexperienced cruisers shouting in panic as they bounced off each other in strong gusts. One boat twice our size lost control, reversed fast towards where we lay helplessly on anchor. I yelled but their boat screamed louder, at full throttle. Smack. Straight into our stern. My girl broken. A fractured rudder. I felt sick. Instead of sailing my dad to Ithaca, *Isean* and I spent the whole of July's searing heat in a mosquito-infested boatyard in Nydri, a tourist town on Lefkas that was unkind from beginning to end.

After weeks of sweaty work, my departure beckoned like a summer dream – breezes at sea, the gentle motion of the water, no more drilling and sanding and climbing down ladders to pee in the night. It wasn't a happy launch, though. Gently put-putting to anchor in neighbouring Tranquil Bay, I was furiously pursued by a speeding boat. One of the brothers who ran the boatyard, shouting about the unsettled bill. He roughly charged alongside and grabbed *Isean* – watch her new paintwork! – as though we were a runaway boat. Such drama! I anchored, as planned, and as he sped off I made a call to the charter company whose responsibility it was to pay. All apologies, Neilson said; their mistake, they'd deal with it. We left, *Isean* and I, while the gruff brothers were having their siesta. I like to think of them rousing, incandescent at our disappearance – '*Malaka*!' – bellowing in rage like one-eyed Polyphemus throwing rocks into the sea. But unlike boastful Odysseus, I left quietly, nothing plundered, no harm done. Their bill was covered, as was always agreed. Still, I felt a frisson of excitement looking back as we escaped Nydri. What joy to be free, to be sailing again, *Isean*'s clean bottom, painted crimson, flying through the water. Like pirates we flew fast away, finally – finally! – to Ithaca.

Rocky Ithaki. Unspoiled and green. Olive groves and fig trees. Cypress and oak. We left the deep navy of the Strait of Ithaca for the palest of blues lapping gently shelving bays. A laid-back little island made more welcome by my need for its solace, its forgiving seabed and friendly people. I hiked its craggy hillsides up to the acropolis of Alalkomenes, and gazed down to the isthmus of Aeotos, where the island spreads north: wooded hills, white surf pounding, the whole scene quietly taking my breath away. Little *Isean* down there waiting for me. And there was Cephalonia, resplendent to the west, better fitting Homer's description of Ithaca: 'farthest out to sea, towards the sunset'. I remembered myself so many years ago, there, looking here. I had never sailed then, didn't know I wanted to. I hadn't known I would find *Isean*. My happy little boat on other adventures with other people. But just after that visit to Greece twenty years ago, I was set on the journey towards her. We were off up to Scotland right away. Outside my parents' house was a little trailer-sailer, a pretty little thing, like a sparrow. It belonged to my brother David. When I asked him about it, without pausing for thought he gave it to me. David is this way. Uniquely kind, a rare soul; the best of us, I often think. I took that little boat back to Brighton and it led to an entirely new life. There were many signs pointing me towards the sea, but this gift from my generous brother was surely the clearest. We cannot conceive of the things that lie ahead. I couldn't have imagined I'd be standing here all these years later, that I'd have arrived in the way that I did, with *Isean*, all those adventures in our wake. All those tempests weathered. Giant creatures below. Fire pouring into sea. Ancient ruined cities we'd sailed over. All those ports, seen for the first time. I felt so lucky. I am lucky. They say you make your own luck, but it's more complicated than that. I was always lucky in finding people to support and encourage me. And I was especially lucky in having an optimistic outlook. A bit of nature, a lot of nurture – thanks, in both cases, to my parents. I had a lot to be grateful for, much to be proud of.

Not long before he died, Stephen told me he was proud of me. I thought it weird at the time. It was unusual, back then, to speak so openly, so directly from the heart, but this wasn't the surprise: Stephen was always comfortable articulating his feelings. What surprised me was that he was proud at all. I had worked in pubs, then shot off to London at nineteen for a job in a bank. Pretty unambitious. Why be proud of something so ordinary? I get it now, though. Sometimes it's the ordinary that's extraordinary, like stars out every night. He was proud that I'd stood on my own two feet, had the courage to leave, to support myself. He understood, at an early age, what counted. Standing up there on Ithaca all those years later, I did feel brave. I felt the courage I see in others achieving the impossible all the time. Things I can't imagine and things I can. Women giving birth. Climbers scaling mountains. People raising children. Speaking up. Falling in love. Getting through depression. Carrying on. We are each of us brave every day. And that courage brings its own rewards. I had mine. I was back in my version of heaven, relishing Ithaca's quiet charm. I swam with colourful fish, washed away the woes of the crash, the negativity it brought. In Vathy, the island's handsome capital, I prepared to leave. Rushing and late with chores, I hurried to haul anchor before the arrival of winds that funnelled up the deep inlet daily. I failed. I was there right before the harbour as the gusts curved up and veered me around like a plaything for the gods' amusement. The statue of Odysseus looked down on me. All right for him, I thought moodily, as I struggled with my chain – he had crew to do the hard work for him. Never mind. I was rushing south to Zakynthos. I'd missed half the summer and I had an important crew member of my own to pick up.

A few days later I was anchored just off the boatyard in Zante town. It's a spot that draws lots of travelling families; some sleeping in vans, some on the ground. There are often kids playing around the fountain, giggling adorably up at you. I stopped in the August heat one afternoon to fill my water bottle and waited as a young woman shampooed her hair. She grinned and handed over her body wash. I wasn't there to wash but was touched by the kindness and joined her, splashing my shoulders in the cool water. It reminded me of my time with the Moken sea nomads in Thailand. The carefree intimacy of women washing on the beach, children running between, splashing and laughing. I spotted a couple of men arrive by dinghy, and said hello, wanting to ask about anchoring. They blanked me. I thought they hadn't heard. 'Excuse me,' I tried again, coming up on their side. They walked faster, averting their heads. They wouldn't even look at me. I was agog, as it hit me that they considered the two of us beneath them. What was freedom to us was vulgar to them. I laughed. I had the luxury of laughing. I hadn't lived with that kind of disdain, didn't know the bitterness and resentment, the hurt, that must surely form in the stomach after years of it. I wondered what they thought I was doing. Selling or begging? Some sort of hustle? I didn't look like a tourist – I seldom did, weaving with gas bottles or fuel cans through holidaymakers in white cotton. I'd almost completely run out of clothes. The few items I had left were clean but hand-washed, perhaps a little stained, maybe with the faint whiff of diesel. I swam and washed every day, but a proper, thorough body-scrubbing hot shower was a rare luxury. My hair was Medusa-like in its tangle of salty spirals. It did get out of hand. I woke up one morning to find a tiny sea urchin on my pillow, my ringlets a magnet for its spikes. On reflection, perhaps those poor men were simply too frightened to look my way. I was a gorgon, a most terrible creature from the deep; I might turn them to stone.

Unusually rude, these men, but I watched with a kind of fascination as my reception changed from place to place. I'd been received with near universal approval in seafaring Brittany, where *Isean*'s diminutive size earned us respect. Often in the Med, where boats are a source of income, I was met with dismissal as people correctly surmised that I had no money to spend. An occasional lack of kindness affected me, when I felt fragile and far from home, but for the most part I didn't take it personally. I had willingly traded places. I'd had a relative amount of influence and power in my life, an existence full of convenience. A comfortable income, a home and the things you surround yourself with, quality products that make you feel a certain way. As time went by, so the expensive things disappeared: a broken speaker I couldn't afford again, a good towel gone overboard, replaced by a cheap flannel. I did not much mourn their loss. My money was better spent on anchor chain to keep me safe. I'd made my life harder, less comfortable, but more rewarding. It was most obvious in how I travelled now. Previous trips away had often been hosted, as a journalist, seeing a region through a rosy filter – you don't see a place at all that way. Now I was on the other extreme: an outsider, living on the periphery of land-based society.

It was an interesting transformation. As appealing as little towns and islands are, there can be an insularity to them that's a bit unforgiving. There are cultural differences, but this is as true in Scotland as it is in Greece. Perhaps it's a clash of personalities. A disconnect between those who leave and those who stay, those who fall outside the mainstream, travelling, living an alternative life, a quiet challenge to the norms. Ordinary working people on the islands were almost always kind, but often, even in the kindest places, my unusual lifestyle – a woman, without husband or children, living on a tiny boat – was considered a bit suspect. I felt it in Portugal, from wives guarding their husbands. I felt it in men wondering at my solitude. I felt it in suspicion from the authorities. In Scotland,

I felt it in the questions from family or neighbours – 'Why don't you sail our islands?' 'Have you fallen out with Scotland?' – as though leaving was a betrayal, a rejection of those left behind. That there was something untrustworthy in my striking out alone. Perhaps this is at the heart of our mistrust of strangers. Who is this person who has abandoned their family? It stretches back to ancient times – when incoming ships often brought trouble – and to myth. Thanks to thundery old Zeus, patron to the stranger, it was a sacred duty to be hospitable to visitors. But the traveller, arriving from sea, was viewed with suspicion. In the oldest of stories this was the case. Take Telemachus, Odysseus's son, seeking news of his father. Sailing to sandy Pylos and a wary welcome from King Nestor: 'Who are you, friends?' You can feel the old king's smile that surely didn't reach his eyes. 'Are you sailing the seas recklessly, like roving pirates, who risk their lives to ruin other people?' I feel you, Telemachus. I came into Pylos on a high too, like Icarus ascending.

There are places where the dominant culture aligns with a particular outlook. The UK's political map turns Conservative blue as you meander along the coasts of Devon and Cornwall. In Italy's impoverished south, I'd found a macho mindset I thought a thing of the past. Later, as I ventured south down the Peloponnese past Pylos, it became noticeable that I was sailing into very conservative territory indeed. It showed even in the small things. In the city of Kalamata, a young woman approached, grave-faced, to warn me about a small rip in my jeans, above the hamstrings, dangerously close to the buttocks. She was so genuinely concerned, so kind, that I thanked her, in the pretence I hadn't known. I watched a man there spend fifteen minutes of his own time straightening an official signpost, as he turned the pavement beneath into an ashtray. Respect for authority over nature. It showed far more in conversations about race and immigration. That region is a heartland of Golden Dawn, Greece's far right, and I found a strong military mindset, a fervour for authority and a deep mistrust of outsiders.

In all of these places I also found much kindness. And I made friends with shared values – as long as I stopped long enough to nurture those friendships. And this was an issue for me. The pull and push of people. I was becoming the ultimate commitment-phobe. 'Remember, she'll leave us,' new friends would joke at my hesitance about future social plans. True, I always had an eye on the sea, always knowing I'd lift anchor when the time was right. All along I'd been tugged between the comfort of friendship and the draw of the sea. And while I love community in theory, in practice it can be stifling – in the cliques and politics, the small-town gossip, the judgements and differences of opinion, and the many many questions. How could I afford to live this way? That echo, all the way from England – how can you just sail away? What then? It's natural to be curious; it's who we are. We imagine trying on a different life. Often, I think, we're looking for the answer we expect. I used to find myself searching for confirmation that this kind of life was beyond my reach. I'd make assumptions: 'This person who did it, they grew up sailing, they were experienced. That person was given a boat, or their parents financed it.' As we often do when we're daunted by something, I was looking for reasons not to try myself. So I recognised the question behind some of the probing. Could I do this? There's no reason why not, I'd always say, if you want to. I was happy to share what I knew, but it could be a bit strange. You don't normally go around fielding detailed questions about how much you earn and spend, what you're doing next. 'Is it the Atlantic crossing?' I have no idea. Perhaps like pregnant women batting strangers' hands off swollen stomachs, my curious lifestyle was deemed a kind of public property.

And perhaps some of those big intrusive questions – 'What are you looking for?' or one memorable 'Are you running from something?' – increased a disquiet that occasionally surfaced, about what my life was now. About who I was. What my purpose was. I wasn't on an odyssey to get back home. I didn't know when my journey would end. Or what, specifically, I was after. It was freedom, sure, but sometimes it felt aimless. It never happened in the wild, but in bays where others splashed in holiday mode, I might question my place. No one wants to be on holiday all the time. Not really. We seem to do better with a balance of occupation and leisure. I could take more pleasure in rest after tasks – cleaning my engine, a bit of writing, language lessons in a winter home. But perhaps that's a response to being in society, the pressure to feel industrious, to fit in. Leaving a port after a period of time brought relief. At sea, the turtles don't care about your status; the sea bream don't ask how you finance your lifestyle; the gulls have no opinion on your future plans. It is all simple again. I always felt light and free when I sailed away. But you can't live forever alone at sea. I was missing the easy company of like-minded friends, the fun of sharing my adventure with my nearest and dearest. Right on cue, an overdue reunion with Saoirse, the most open-minded and big-hearted youngster of all. That huge grin and jaunty little stride heading towards me in Zante town. 'Yo, Smillie!' Back to shared meals and beers and laughs, Saoirse's exceptionally good vegan cooking, our conversations about life and love, politics and community. And back to sniping over her lackadaisical approach to my most cherished ritual.

'Saoirse, are you making my tea in an unwashed cup?'
'I was saving you water! You're always moaning about water.'

'No!! You can't take shortcuts with tea! You only need a
tiny bit to clean it!'

Saoirse wedges herself in, skilfully balancing the boiled
kettle as *Isean* bounces through waves. She pours, then
chats, until I can bear it no longer.

'It's going to stew! Put some milk in! Take the teabag
out!'

Saoirse glares out, silently hands me half a cup of astrin-
gent tea. I eye the tannin-rich liquid, brown as tar with a
film of scum. The air is heavy as I taste.

'Mmmm. It's. Well. It's bitter. Maybe more sugar will
help.'

Saoirse shakes her head, laughing. 'Tea wanker.'

'Biscuit?'

She unpacked. A tiny cabin bag, full of stuff for me. Teabags,
check. Chocolate. Yep. Books and a new speaker for my birthday. And the biggest treat of all: a flush valve replacement for
my broken toilet. For herself, she brought little more than the
clothes she stood in, fitting seamlessly with my minimal style.
Really, I have the best pals.

We set south, where the clumsy flotillas don't go. We visited
Olympia, paid respects at the Temple of Zeus and were
rewarded with perfect conditions, favourable winds and a following sea. I put Saoirse in charge and she skippered us expertly
to the uninhabited island of Proti, her first passage completed,
a giant leap from St Alban's tidal race. I consulted the charts for
the onward journey with my dad in mind. The boat crash had
cancelled his Ithaca trip; I'd scope out Pylos as an alternative.
Sandy Pylos, home of King Nestor. In this place where Telemachus had sought news of his father, I too hoped for paternal
reunion. On the chart, I noticed an omega bay just north of the
town. 'Let's stop on the way,' I said – there were no pictures,

but from the shape it had potential to be pretty. A wild under-estimation. Voidokilia Beach is a paradise. Entirely unspoiled. No rows of loungers, no tavernas; just clear Ionian waters lapping a horseshoe beach where turtles hatch. The ruins of an ancient castle and, sure enough, piles upon piles of silky white dunes. We anchored in flat aquamarine under the Cave of Nestor. It was the end of August, the beach still busy with locals and tourists, children splashing excitedly in the warm water. It had that last-gasp-of-summer feeling, everyone soaking it up. We swung in the middle of the bay as the sun sank. The outer tips of the crescent beach fell into shade and people gradually drew to its centre. Saoirse glanced back and smiled. I followed her eye. Everyone, to a man, woman and child, was standing quietly in one precious beam of light, staring out at the golden ball before us – all of us joined together in a moment of silent awe.

The next morning we sailed a stone's throw – three miles – round into Navarino Bay, a vast natural shelter where Pylos town sits. I was unprepared for how beautiful it would be. The island of Sphacteria marks the entrance, and we passed between it and Tsichli-Baba – an islet with a natural arch, twisted rock formations jutting out of the sea, pulling the eye up. A drama of cliffs and caves, a haunting atmosphere that makes you feel like an explorer, the first to see it. Empty golden coves off to port, another castle to starboard, and in the distance, Pylos, its silver church dome glinting in the morning sun. There was an abandoned marina tucked off to its east, a few boats anchored outside. And even from this distance, I knew. I could feel it. 'I've found home,' I told Saoirse. We did a quick recce – great bakeries, cafés and gelaterias in the lively harbour square. A few polite Dutch and German tourists, vastly outnumbered by retired Greeks. A one-hour bus ride to the city of Kalamata, where Saoirse could fly home – and Cat, already packing my teabags, could fly in. A perfect wintering spot. I was thrilled. A phone call home, a little studio booked for my dad's visit, but first, a couple of weeks to explore the very southern tip of mainland Greece.

The Peloponnese is glove-shaped, its fingers stretching between the Ionian and Aegean Seas. *Isean* and I ran south round the first headland to pleasant Koroni, then east into the Mani peninsula. Or as I like to think of it now, the middle finger. It is a wildly inhospitable place to sail. You feel like a toy boat against massive cliffs, looking for protection from strong winds that rush between two seas. There isn't much. It is barren. Talk to Greeks about Mani and they laugh that the people there are a bit special, clannish, perhaps a little fierce – modern Maniots claim lineage to the Spartans. When you spend time in this isolated area you understand that its people would have had to be strong and independent to survive, even in modern times. Roads only came here in the 1970s. It is cut off from the rest of Greece by a colossal mountain range, the Taygetus. The saddest of slopes, Mount Taygetus, where weak Spartan newborns were left exposed to die, the scholars said. Piracy was once rife here too. Incomers beware. I sailed along, staring up and out to a sea that stretches to Libyan shores. And near there is Cape Tenaro, an entrance to Hades. I know. Another one. But here, in this place of bleak beauty, where the winds howl, and shelter is rare, I can believe it. Here, you can feel deep isolation, and here it feels true.

In choppy waters, I reached Mezapos and its perfect circular anchorage. I didn't know it, but this minuscule natural harbour is thought to be Telepylos, where Homer's Laistrygonians smashed Odysseus's fleet with boulders. It's a legend that inspires pity when you're there, given the violent history of the region, for it must have looked like such a rare thing – a refuge on this unfriendliest of coastlines – and it probably wasn't much more welcoming in real life. When I blew in, there was heavy swell but inside the harbour was flat calm. The charts showed four metres, a perfect depth for anchoring. But I was too nervous to enter. It was windy and the place was tiny. I feared rocks – in the water, rather than raining down from an ambush above, although who knows. Maybe it was my gut warning me. I like the idea that water has memory. Whatever caused my foreboding, like Odysseus, I stayed outside. I had a terrible night thrown around in waves, although admittedly not as bad as he did, losing eleven boats and most of his men to giant cannibals.

On the eastern side of the finger lies Gytheio, once the port of Sparta. From where beautiful Helen left for Troy, from Menelaus to the arms of Paris, by will or otherwise. Her face launched a thousand ships, they say, supposedly sparking a war men wanted for glory. A treacherous place, it turned out. Here I met coastguards on a random check. Giorgios, all machismo and designer shades. I was unfortunate enough to witness his bad boat-handling; his pride was bruised, his temper in full swing. 'Malaka,' was how he greeted me, his colleague looking apologetic and embarrassed. Looking for fault, he discovered my batteries disconnected. 'You're not going anywhere any more,' he said triumphantly. *Isean* would be impounded. It was a trap worse than Telepylos; several boats already lay seized in Gytheio harbour, some of them suspected trafficking vessels, some unfortunate sailors with minor typos on their paperwork. Batteries hurriedly reconnected, I escaped his clutches and away we fled to collect Cat in Kalamata. I anchored off the seafront – *forbidden!* – was sent to an oversized ship's quay, almost crushing my head in my efforts to find something to tie to as port officers stood watching. My smiling *'Neró?'* elicited a gruff response. 'NO water!' If I thought I'd left the sullen coastguards behind in southern Italy, I had another think coming. '*Efcharistó!*' I responded brightly. Thank you. It was something my brother had taught me. When I was little, a certain neighbour would glower past in animosity for some unknowable reason. She made me so nervous. 'Good morning, Betty,' Stephen would chirp, shocking her into a smile in return. I'd thought it terribly clever, a Trojan horse — the element of surprise! I deployed this tactic, beaming through officers' stern questions, sometimes even cracking that blue steel, but it was usually impossible to get a human response from the authorities. I grew weary of trying. Most often I'd be polite and distant; sometimes I'd be as sullen as them. I wasn't deferential, which probably irked those attracted to the power of the role. When they were particularly rude, I'd be over-the-top friendly in my thank-yous and painted Joker grin. I'd taken friendly to extremes. Weaponised it. It didn't help me. Humans, like all animals, are adept at reading body language, and my fake smiles barely masked my resentment. It was the coastguard's job to check boats at sea. I was in their territory, sailing a course fast growing in popularity with human traffickers. The Calabrian Route, as it's called, stretches west from Turkey, past the fingers of the Peloponnese to the toe of southern Italy. Private sailing boats not much bigger than mine were stolen for the purpose, crammed with vulnerable people below deck. I knew I looked suspicious to these men, as a woman alone at sea. As unjust as it was, the hostility I encountered was unsurprising; in the context, understandable even. I didn't want to become embittered — it would only make me a more suspicious character. And I didn't want to feel this way! I was out there sailing for the joy and freedom. If our man Socrates was right about the risks to ourselves of perpetrating wrong, then meeting injustice with candour surely nurtures our well-being. We respond in kind; even at our most hostile, we can be disarmed by warmth. This thing that Stephen had been good at still eluded me. How to stay open in the face of opposition. It's a hard one. We like people who like us. Who are like us. That's natural. They're easy to like. It's more useful to find common ground with those who challenge us. Because there are people all over the place we clash with. How to reach each other through conflict? If I wanted this, one of the hardest lessons of all, life was about to oblige.

That crash, just north of Ithaca, had put *Isean* and me on a different heading. We were set on a collision course with Nic, a young French sailor I'd met in Sardinia. He heard about the accident and, in generosity, paused his journey to help me in the boatyard back in Lefkas. He became a good friend. He had also followed the route south to the Peloponnese. It was a path that would end in disaster for him. Cat and I joined him in a taverna in the tiny village of Finikounda, where he was drawn into rounds of strong tsipouros – *Yamas!* – with locals. It ended messily, him drunk and shouting, out of reach and angry beyond reason. A late-night disturbance in a sleepy place. He untied his boat and went off to anchor in the bay before disappearing below deck, presumably to pass out. Back on the quay, Cat and I were relieved; finally everything was calm. But in the meantime, the Pylos port police had been called. It was quiet when they motored out to his boat. The officers shouted through a megaphone: no response. Moments later, through the dark we heard screaming: Nic, crying, 'I was sleeping.' I rowed out frantically on my dinghy. By the time I got there, Nic was handcuffed and sobbing, a gun at his head. The atmosphere was heavy with violence, the air so charged you could taste it. He was screaming, they were screaming. I was quietly terrified. It was the worst kind of emotional, the most dangerous kind. 'Leave immediately!' – a high-pitched shriek at me. 'You are obstructing us.' There was no room for more screaming, for anger or ego, for right or wrong. No time for anything other than pure instinct. In desperation, I took the hand of the officer near me, the one who didn't have his rifle raised. And I pleaded. 'Let me help.' The atmosphere softened. 'You can help lift anchor,' he said, allowing me to board. I sat against Nic, the weapon now aimed at both of us. 'He is handcuffed.' I was close to tears. 'Please stop.' The gun went down. I could have cried with relief. We think we have no power. But it's not true. We can always reach out. We have the gift of being human in a human situation, with the power to connect.

They took Nic away in handcuffs. I didn't see much more of Cat; we moored *Isean* in Pylos harbour and I spent her visit with lawyers in a Kalamata courtroom. The defence went unheard; Nic would end up with a four-year prison sentence for resisting arrest and – they claimed – threatening the port police. Sentenced and released on appeal, he sailed into Pylos ahead of a storm. The town where he'd been held. I watched his arrival with a heavy heart; there are conditions other than weather that make entry to a port dangerous. Cat left and my dad arrived. A long overdue visit at a troubled time. We found Nic in the minimart, alone and fragile, clearly homesick. Young for his twenty-nine years, and in serious trouble, he cut a sorrowful sight. Sam went over, shook his hand, started singing the French national anthem. Nic joined in, the two of them smiling, strains of the Marseillaise surreally rising out of the cheese aisle. Such a strange and touching sight. My big-hearted dad. The gesture just about broke my heart.

We took Nic under our wing. The three of us went to ancient Messini, wandered the Sanctuary of Asclepius and lingered in the amphitheatre. My dad sang – Paul Robeson, of course, 'Joe Hill', the union anthem for the Industrial Workers of the World. A small crowd of visitors gathered from around the ancient city to applaud him. Amongst them, a pair of appreciative American 'wobblies'. Sam was utterly delighted. Then home for dinner in his little garden apartment. A truly special day. But as we walked back to our boats later, Nic and I were being watched in the dark. Two off-duty port police in an unmarked car. The officer who had processed him in jail. He lifted his shirt to reveal the gun tucked into his trousers. Erratically, he paced, barking orders. 'On one foot, stand. Arms out!' Suddenly, his trigger finger at Nic's temple. 'You should have been shot that night.' He took me aside, talked of protection – this man, leaning close, excited, in the dark, with his gun. He was trying to open my eyes. It was something age-old. I was like him; Nic was other. 'He's not French,' he kept saying. 'Look at his face.' A reference, I understood, to Nic's Asian features. Without hope of success, I tried again to connect, a role that seems often to fall to women caught up in the violence of men. They toyed with us for a terrifying hour. The following morning we sat in my dad's apartment, writing down what happened. 'Look at his face,' Nic said, mimicking the officer. 'He's not French,' we parroted. Shock or bravado, our way of coping. Laughing, I looked at my dad. He looked like he could cry. I stared at the floor. It was how I felt. A new kind of low, this perspective. We left for the lawyers – what a holiday – on the way diverted to the underworld, the prehistoric caves of Diros on that forbidding Mani peninsula. We made our way down into nature's cathedral, where it was cool and silent and still, and we floated on the lake that wound unseen through labyrinth tunnels, waxy with stalactites. The boatman's paddle, my dad's voice drifting softly in song. Safe down there.

On my dad's birthday, we persuaded Nic to go. We left with him. Both boats anchored under Nestor's cave, golden jackals howling in the moonlight. The first time I'd taken my dad sailing, his first night ever sleeping on *Isean*. Not the circumstances I'd have chosen, but all the more memorable for the extreme highs rising out of deep lows. What powerfully strange times:

everything raw and intense, beauty persisting through the bleakness, love always there. We saw Nic a good way north and then turned back. I felt immediately lighter, unburdened in the knowledge that he was safe and gone. I will never forget that sail back to sandy Pylos with my dad. Skies aflame with sunset, us full of joy. Music blaring, stamping in time as *Isean* bounded through Homeric seas turning wine-dark with nightfall. Navarino Bay. We rounded that beautiful entrance, its twisted rocks looming, the sky raining stars. No stress, I gybed the sail; I knew this path well, nothing would go wrong. We were singing our hearts out, my dad and I, the harmonies echoed in the caves we sailed past. The memories were precious; they would need to be. Soon after, I would find myself alone in Pylos, locked down in a global pandemic and the only witness in a serious complaint against the town's police. An uneasy time. I always had an eye out for that unmarked car as I walked to *Isean* in the dark. I'd picked up heavy baggage that would have made it wiser to leave. But the Fates were against me. In November I injured my back. In December I broke my foot. *Isean* started our Greek odyssey with a fractured rudder; I ended the year with a fractured foot. Me and my girl. In sync as ever.

Off she goes. Hobbling home for Christmas. Back to her kind. Just as well; she's not exactly nimble on board, dragging that big medical boot around. She tripped on a pavement! Wheesht! Land can be dangerous for a sailor! I shouldn't laugh. First, she hurt her back. Of course she did! Stress. Human stuff. Tight chest, shallow breathing. Her holding, all wrong. The broken foot was bad timing, though. Now we can't leave. I can keep her safe at sea, but I can't help her here.

She's small in this harbour. Trapped with toy soldiers. Badges and buttons. Big boots marching. By day and by night. Eyes in dark shades. Searching and staring. Spitting and swaggering. Hooting and whistling. She's quiet here. A caged bird, wings clipped. I feel it too. For me and for her. I am a boat, but sometimes I'm a mother, rocking her to sleep.

I'm sitting proud. She flew farther than she knew, this fledgling. We'll fly again. Off by spring. Better broken foot than broken wing. Better that she's gone. She'll come back strong. I'll take her to the wild. It's what she needs. Windows free of walls. No lights drowning dreams. There at sea she drifts off with life all around. Surrounded by love. Fish knocking. Birds calling. Shy sea horses, tails holding tails. And come creatures bigger than me. Giants circling in the night. What she can't see she feels. She knows the peace of it. Dreams of it. I know she'll return to it. Back to me, back home, us back to sea. Back to the mothership.

14.

I lay on my back in the den I made, my book perched like a little tent on my stomach. I stared at my bamboo roof and listened to a tapping sound — a carpenter bee inside one of the canes, I decided. I'd been lost in thought and it was late in the day. We were in the sunset hour, that soft quality of light beaming through the gaps, painting everything in tiger stripes of gold and shade. The water had turned from jade to olive, as the light bounced off the posidonia beds beneath. This secret place, hidden from view by vertiginous cliffs, slate-grey and burnt orange. As always, I meant to come for a few hours and stayed all day. Just one more swim, I'd think, then a coffee, maybe some reading. The hours drifted. Time passed companionably, somehow, despite my being alone. Maybe it was the familiarity of the shipping forecast from the radio on the shelf, the books, like friends lined up alongside. The ravens calling, lizards rustling, waves lapping. It was all of it — the sounds, the shelf, the bamboo roof. It was the beauty of the natural setting, but it was also that I'd made it, this place, with things I'd found and brought. My den had that happy peaceful atmosphere that makes you feel safe and well, like a sun-dappled reading room. Like home. I looked out over Navarino Bay, to the islands and rocks silhouetted in the sinking sun, and I felt utterly content.

The pandemic had come and I had returned, from London to *Isean* — naturally, she was my bubble. At sea, as on land, movement was banned; we couldn't sail. The strangest thing for us, so used to freedom, to be trapped. Tied to concrete, claustrophobic and overlooked. I had started to feel lonely, far from family and friends. I was used to being alone – but not feeling alone. I had to act, to make an effort to be happy. I had sought out this stony little cove, the kind most people ignore. The kind I love best. Strewn with pebbles and flotsam, mounds of dried sea-weed, boulders and rocks, twisted and pitted. They're the kind of places Maw Joss took my cousin Lorraine and me as children – smears of muddy shoreline, fragmented rocky coves along the River Clyde, where we ran out of the freezing water to flasks of tea and crisps. Yellow Rock Bay, I called it. A messy spit of shore, backed by a tangle of wild flowers, red berries with green hearts climbing, the eponymous rock. I exchanged gloomy anxious days, filled with news of the daily death rate, for days alone and barefoot on sand and seaweed. It was not far, but it felt a world away from the concrete structures and orderly lines of boats in Pylos harbour.

From there I could see everything – the patrol boat coming and going – but no one could see me. My bamboo roof blended into the rocks. I knew that it was hidden well, because I looked for it when I swam. Though it was banned, I swam. There was no one to see me float, no one to hear my happy splashes. I loved the ritual of going every day. Down this overgrown rutted track, the drops and ledges, branches for balance, springy limbs on a slippery ravine. Happy reminders of teenage days exploring crags and hills around Dumbarton, in trouble for staying out late. I was reminded of that here, with an adult's agency to bend the rules. I spent illegal hours over the daily allowance, hidden away. Time stolen in nature, like Orwell's Winston in search of fleeting freedom in the Golden Country.

And this quiet place held me when sadness overwhelmed; I cried on the shore, matriarchal ravens watching from the cliffs. The pandemic had aggravated scars, thrown the soft blurred lines of past grief into hard sharp focus. Anyone who has experienced loss will remember the familiarity those first days brought – of waking already in the knowledge that something big is wrong. We were now in late spring, a time already full of memory and loss – of Lorraine, of my mum, of Stephen. The pain was amplified and complicated, cut off from loved ones in a crisis. But like any crisis, once we are in it, we get through it; we cope, we learn and we grow. What I knew about times of crisis was that they had the potential to be very special. That we could surprise ourselves with what we could face. And I knew that, above all, I had to look after myself. It was like a klaxon in my head, a call from my mum, a reminder on coping. After Stephen died, we took our turns at falling apart, one of us always there to catch the other. Our anguish eventually bled into the humdrum of daily life as we tried to find our way back to normality. One time my dad came indoors to find my mum dissolved in tears. 'Can you wait ten minutes, love,' he'd asked kindly, holding her. 'I've cement to pour.' She stood open-mouthed, then laughed. 'Right enough, I better just get on.' She loved that story. I was reminded daily of her way of coping, of how she taught me to cope too, to be strong. Cry, help each other through, but then get outside, lighten things, remember to be hopeful and happy, and finally, be brave. 'We'll get there,' she always said. And I was trying. We all were.

I was sitting amongst driftwood and bamboo when I had the idea of making a shelter. It would be a different kind of shelter, though. The safety it would provide – its truest purpose – would be in its making. It was a way of looking after myself. Cutting and lashing the bamboo; tying the clove hitches; finding the beams, flat rocks for a floor; scouring the wilderness, the bracken and leaves, seaweed and twigs underfoot releasing oils and scents. Without knowing why, I felt better, my body soothed, my mind occupied, tasks filling the place that was sometimes empty. Hours turned into days and then weeks; I was the world's slowest castaway. But then, why rush? Spring, not the subtlest of seasons, was making itself felt. I was awed by the ever-changing colours, in thrall to the ravens, though they didn't seem to like me back, judging by their hectoring and grunting; probably the spirit of Maw Joss.

I bridged two rocks with a beam for my bamboo roof, then I'd sit there, whittling wood in the shade. I had my flask of coffee, sandwiches. I had a purpose to my days. It was a sanctuary and adventure at once, like *Isean*. Perhaps it took me back to the hut where Lorraine and I slept in Maw Joss's back garden. We kept a tin of biscuits there and I remember the excitement when my gran's friends indulged us with a visit. I swelled with pride, passing the biscuit tin like I'd seen adults do. Playing house. In the cove, I made more shelves. I didn't need shelves – of course I didn't – but when I placed my little library, when I hung my bikini from the bamboo hook, I was filled with such delight at these comforts of home I kept going. I found the smooth limb of a tree – with one side branch, it looked like a giant prairie cactus – and dug it in, an aesthetic addition for its exotic castaway feel. It was meant as a coat stand, but like the bamboo 'decking', the galangal frog and the Stone Age dumb-bells – two holed rocks on a bamboo cane – its main purpose was to make me laugh.

The weeks of scavenging suited me well. Bin-diving, effectively, but on my castaway beach I could describe it in more romantic terms. Beachcombing: rescuing things washed ashore or cast aside. Like the expensive canteen of cutlery some-one discarded – a painful reminder, perhaps, of a love story gone wrong. One day I was unspeakably excited to find an elab-orate trunk lid – tin and wood, red and green, shiny treasure that found its way into my fantasy. A wonderland in the wild. As the flotsam and jetsam drifted ashore, I was reminded that we made things as kids – wooden peg dolls, my cardboard box theatre. I was back to that creative freedom, finding natural things – a heart-shaped leaf, a stone with a hole worn through – and making them into homeware. It was all so pleasing. I didn't care how corny it was, I hung that love heart up in my den. Then I found a pile of heart-shaped leaves around the entrance, a gift scattered from above. Even as I played castaway, though, part of me was uncomfortable with this childish commodification of nature, my hearts and flowers, shelves and cushions. Like planting a flag in the ground, this human need to make a corner of nature mine. Disrupting life all around as I crashed through shelters other creatures had built – a perfect web, beautifully spun, a 'wee-bit heap o' leaves an' stibble' in the words of a favourite Robert Burns poem: 'To a Mouse, On turning her up in her Nest, with the Plough.' Unearthing stones, I caused a mass exodus of the insects that lived there, tiny slaters, beetles, spiders, all running frantically for cover, their world destroyed. 'An' cozie here, beneath the blast, thou thought to dwell, till crash! the cruel coulter past out thro' thy cell.' It broke my heart a little.

The carpenter bees were back, oily black violet. I noticed them buzzing around the prairie tree, inspecting this new addition to the area, then they moved in. I felt guilty – it would fall over in the first brisk breeze. As I wondered how to make it more stable, my eye was drawn to a tiny worm making its way up a rock. Closer inspection revealed it was dead, carried by industrious ants, marching in formation to their colony at the top. Its segmented body glided upwards in an S. The beam I had put up for my roof had given them a bridge and I was pleased that this interference seemed helpful. But then, what do I know of their lives? We only recently learned that ants are farmers too. We are just beginning to learn that our intelligence is not the only form, that we are not the only species capable of planning, of having memory, feelings. At that little cove, buzzing with activity, I regained the fascination for insects I once had. I just needed the time to stop and look. This is what children know and we have forgotten.

I slept there sometimes, staring out over the still water as the moon wandered the sky. Like being back on anchor. The closest I could get to being at sea with *Isean*. How I missed it. By June, things began to open up. Soon we'd be sailing again. The thought of that! While I played on the shore like a child, *Isean* had been stuck in a stifling harbour, closed up. Growing a garden underneath, stuffy inside. She needed air, she needed to move. We both did. I wanted to be back out there, to dolphins and turtles greeting our days, to crystal waters, caves and castles, mountain ranges and wooded hills. Back to an incredible life lived on the cheap. I was ready. I was positive and happy. And strong. This was important. As wonderful as life is at sea, it is hardly trouble-free. I'd once joked that I was practising survival skills for a coming apocalypse, sailing around looking for water and places to hide. But things had actually started to feel a bit apocalyptic. In sailing out into the world – not even very far at that – the problems had been bigger than I'd imagined. There had been different challenges to those I'd expected. You can't anticipate all the setbacks, but as a sailor you plan and you mitigate, consider solutions. It's a natural consequence of being far from the safety of land, just a few planks of wood separating you from drowning. You learn to think about conditions in the short and long term – these winds against that tide will create waves. The storm to the west will send swell. Spring tides, neap tides, next summer's trade winds. Weather fronts and currents moving around the globe. People moving too. Patterns. Patterns changing. Patterns destabilising. What we know in thinking ahead is that things will likely get harder. What we also know is that in such times, things also flourish and grow. That humans are often astonishing, that in facing a problem, we can make something better than we had before. That we can find the best in ourselves and help each other through.

I considered direction. Where would be affordable and safe in another pandemic wave. Where best for peace, and where in pursuit of happiness? Do I turn left to the south or right to the north? Is it east towards Turkey, or west back to Italy. South to Tunisia. Or give Greece a chance? One thing was clear, I couldn't evade the man-made stuff of land, the problems, checks and rules. I wasn't a little by-the-wind sailor that could drift around oceans forever snacking. I wasn't a woman–boat hybrid flying above the heads of the authorities. I might have sea creatures residing in my tangled mop, but I couldn't actually petrify the men who gave me trouble at sea. Medusa-mad hair aside, I was a recognisable part of the human race, and that was unavoidable. Even if the patrol boats were not on my immediate horizon, they would be in the back of my mind, curbing my sense of freedom. On the other hand, wasn't that up to me?

> Laistrygonians, Cyclops,
> wild Poseidon – you won't encounter them
> unless you bring them along inside your soul,
> unless your soul sets them up in front of you.

Perhaps the freedom was in me. In my response. In where I chose to focus. In remembering what I've known all along, about joy in the moment. It's impossible to outsail the hard stuff of life, the world we've made, the storms that blow through it. The freedom comes in setting the tiller and the storm sail, in getting through still flying. I felt strong and optimistic, calm and confident, capable of dealing with whatever was coming my way. This feeling – like all others – would not last forever, but I would run with it while it did.

There was a more permanent shift too. In all of my roaming, I had felt a change taking place inside, a return to the person I really was. Something of that kid I'd once been. And this version of me, the truest perhaps, was the one I liked best. As hard as things had been in Pylos – perhaps because things had been so hard – that had accelerated. We often talk about our ego, protecting the child inside. I don't much like the language but I recognise the truth of that inner child, the inexplicable hurt feelings that rise up sometimes, unstoppable on their route to a half-remembered injustice. But surely it goes two ways. That inner child – like all children – is more resilient than we realise. More resilient, sometimes, than our adult selves. Sometimes it's the child who has the better coping mechanisms. In Pylos, that kid protected me, the little happy curly-headed one that sang to the geese and played with the stars. 'To hell with adulting when it's this miserable,' she said. And I'd responded, escaped, sought adventure and fun. I took the idea of being isolated and trapped and really ran with it, off to play in some mad Robinson Crusoe fantasy. Eccentric as hell, but she was right. I'd kept myself safe and happy. While the world shut down, while everyone was struggling, I was lost in a wild wonderland. I hadn't just got through hard times, I'd thrived. I thought I knew about happiness, but I'm still learning. With almost nothing, I learned to be happier than I thought possible. I learned that it was not sacrifice, but freedom to need less. I learned to accept when happiness isn't there, to trust in it coming back. I saw that resilience brings happiness, overcoming fear brings joy. I learned the most important thing of all – that it can take an effort to be happy. It's easy to feel joy when everything is nice, but to find it in storms, what a triumph it is then.

One sunny July day in Pylos, I found myself ready to go. Freedom. Time to choose it again. Shake off the nerves, stretch the old muscles. *La farfalla*, I said to *Isean*. A butterfly sail to end this strange chrysalis. Nine months in harbour, a long gestation. North of the bay, a shakedown sail and I needed it. I was clumsy and wobbly. Fluttering and flapping. Tripping on shackles, entangled in lines, *Isean* swaying in disbelief. 'Look at the state of you!' No problem, I patted her hatch. 'Wheesht, *Isean*!' She'd soon feel like an extension of myself again. We'd been through a lot – battered by storms, by fractures and crashes; left high and dry. We'd been locked up here and thrown out there. Always the two of us. Through all my mistakes she had never once let me down. She never would. How I loved her. How I missed her! Back in the wild. Physically I knew it. Even in my sleep I felt it. My soul responded to it. The air around us. The water gurgling. No motors revving, no boots marching. Not being watched. Just being. Stars shining. Tumbling into my berth, waking up. Sunlight streaming in. The peace of it. The delicious space of it. We anchored at the cove, a little farewell. Butterflies fluttering where my final brunch was set – all fancy silverware laid out on the treasure chest. A mad hatter's tea party if ever there was one. It had been extraordinarily healing, this little place, taking me back in time and holding me through a crisis. But *Isean* had waited long enough for me to stop playing castaway.

I waded through waves, smiled in soft sand. Watching her. At sea she comes alive. Swinging free. No lines to hold her down. No rules to keep me there. I rowed and found her back to herself. My brilliant friend, riding white horses in the wind. The waves flowed along her waterline, like forward momentum. Sailing herself. She was off without me! 'Wait, *Isean*!' I jumped on board. Up for adventure. Up with the anchor and unfurl the sails. We headed out to that twisted entrance – finally a place of departure. We flew, a dead run out of the underworld. Goose-winged, as I prefer it. I sang as we left, the sails filled in chorus, like birdsong at dawn. We survived the night! I didn't look back. I'd left a sign to show we might return. Painted on the wall. Something hopeful left in our place. *Isean*, it said, in shining silver, a little bird above.

Acknowledgements

In memory of Jeff Howlett, who taught me all my favourite things and changed the course of my life. Of Tjoppe, the most generous of sailors and of men, who left too suddenly and too soon. And of beautiful Bersita, who always knew how to fly.

Much of this book was written on the move and was indelibly shaped by people and place. To all those who opened homes and hearts to me – thank you. Eleni and Stavros for my beautiful bird room in the eaves in Kalamata, Jules (and Dimitra) at Dio Pigadia farm for love and support during hard times in Pylos, Alex and Eugenia for the same in Paleros. Lise Autogena and the ace community at Hermitage Pier on the Thames, for berths, friendship and inspiration in the London fog. Merryn Owen, Matthew Kenyon, Heleen Arps and so many excellent neighbours upriver at Greenland Dock. My dear friend Claire Soper for opening Matthew's precious studio to me, Audrey Gillan for Glasgow hospitality, and Jules Morgan for the same in Southsea. Felicity Cloake and her cairn terrier Wilf for grudgingly sharing his bed with me. To Manda and Carolann, who read early drafts and cheered me on, and especially to the wise and wonderful Frederica Notley, who read several (and Captain Lila and Quinn, London's premier circus double act). A major thank you to my former boss at the *Guardian*, Malik Meer, for taking a punt and giving me my first serious shot at writing, also at the newspaper, Suzie Worroll and Steve Chamberlain for support on the journey. To my agent David Godwin for the necessary kick to get on with this strange little book. Paula Flanagan (for making it flow), Nick Lowndes (for skills and saintly patience), and the rest of the exceptional editing team at Michael Joseph, thanks – of course – for insightful editing, but especially for encouragement and understanding as life dealt some left-field cards along the way. Thanks too for saving me from myself countless times – any embarrassments that remain are entirely my own. Thanks to Liv Thomas, Jennifer Breslin and the rest of the publicity team for tireless work, boundless enthusiasm and creative ideas. Thank you to Lauren Wakefield and Ella Ginn for gracing my story with such a beautiful cover. And a special thank you to my editor, Dan Bunyard, who saw, right from the beginning, what the book could be and who gave me the time, freedom and support to make it so. I hope I did. Thank you to Roseanne and Conrad, Isla and family, Christine, Agnes, Elaine and Moh, and so many others for support at home in Scotland. To Sam and David for trusting me with our story. And to Wolfi – thank you for the new beginning.